10 Moral Paradoxes

Saul Smilansky is a professor in the Department of Philosophy at the University of Haifa, Israel. He is the author of the widely acclaimed book *Free Will and Illusion* (2000) and has published articles in many of the leading philosophical journals.

10 Moral Paradoxes

Saul Smilansky

Blackwell
Publishing

© 2007 by Saul Smilansky

BLACKWELL PUBLISHING
350 Main Street, Malden, MA 02148–5020, USA
9600 Garsington Road, Oxford OX4 2DQ, UK
550 Swanston Street, Carlton, Victoria 3053, Australia

The right of Saul Smilansky to be identified as the Author of this
Work has been asserted in accordance with the UK Copyright,
Designs, and Patents Act 1988.

First published 2007 by Blackwell Publishing Ltd

1   2007

Library of Congress Cataloging-in-Publication Data

Smilansky, Saul.
  10 moral paradoxes / Saul Smilansky.
     p. cm.
  Includes bibliographical references and index.
  ISBN 978-1-4051-6086-5 (hardcover : alk. paper)
  ISBN 978-1-4051-6087-2 (pbk. : alk. paper)
  1. Ethics.   2. Paradox.   I. Title.   II. Title: Ten moral paradoxes.

  BJ1031.S625   2007
  170—dc22
                                                    2006028203

A catalogue record for this title is available from the British Library.

Set in 10.5/13pt Galliard
by Graphicraft Limited, Hong Kong
Printed and bound in Singapore
by COS Printers Pte Ltd

The publisher's policy is to use permanent paper from mills that
operate a sustainable forestry policy, and which has been manufactured
from pulp processed using acid-free and elementary chlorine-free
practices. Furthermore, the publisher ensures that the text paper and
cover board used have met acceptable environmental accreditation
standards.

For further information on Blackwell Publishing, visit our website:
www.blackwellpublishing.com

Well, the way of paradoxes is the way of truth. To test Reality we must see it on the tightrope. When the Verities become acrobats we can judge them.

Oscar Wilde, *The Picture of Dorian Gray*

The gods too are fond of a joke.

Aristotle

For Jonathan

Contents

	List of Figures	viii
	Acknowledgments	ix
	Introduction	1
1	Fortunate Misfortune	11
2	The Paradox of Beneficial Retirement	23
3	Two Paradoxes about Justice and the Severity of Punishment	33
4	Blackmail: The Solution	42
5	The Paradox of Non-Punishment	50
6	On Not Being Sorry about the Morally Bad	59
7	Choice-Egalitarianism and the Paradox of the Baseline	67
8	Morality and Moral Worth	77
9	The Paradox of Moral Complaint	90
10	Preferring Not to Have Been Born	100
11	A Meta-Paradox: Are Paradoxes Bad?	113
12	Reflections on Moral Paradox	122
	Postscript: The Future and Moral Paradox	134
	References	138
	Index	142

List of Figures

2.1 Excellent chance that a replacement for someone
from the professionally worst group will be better   25
3.1 Disparity between the required severity of
punishment and deserved mitigation   36
3.2 Some possible levels of punishment   39
7.1 The world according to choice-egalitarianism   73

List of Figures

Acknowledgments

Paradox is the poison flower of quietism, the iridescent sheen of a putrefied mind, the greatest depravity of all.
Thomas Mann, *The Magic Mountain*

Since so many people assisted in my pursuit of paradox over the years, let's hope that Thomas Mann was mistaken. But, in any case, I am grateful to those who read and commented, at various stages, on this book or on the essays from which it emerged. I have tried to keep track of this beneficence, and apologize to anyone whom I might have forgotten.

Many gave me helpful comments on drafts of one or more of the original papers, or of their rewritten versions. These include Shlomit Baruch, Dan Bein, Aaron Ben-Zeev, Avner de-Shalit, David Enoch, Galia Geist, Amihud Gilead, Michael Gross, Meir Hemmo, David Heyd, Giora Hon, Doug Husak, Hagar Kahana-Smilansky, Iddo Landau, James Lenman, Kasper Lippert-Rasmussen, Tal Manor, Jeff McMahan, Ariel Meirav, Merav Mizrahi, Jacob Ross, Simon Rubin, Eli Salzberger, Jonathan Seglow, Jonathan Smilansky, Daniel Statman, Hillel Steiner, Larry Temkin, and Eddy Zemach.

I would also like to mention a category of persons who necessarily remain anonymous, an academic version of the Tomb of the Unknown Soldier: the referees for the journals that accepted my papers and, occasionally, the referees for the unmentionable journals that rejected papers; such referees (as well as editors) frequently made good suggestions. I cannot hope to mention all of the people who gave me comments on my papers after they had been published. I would, however, like to note with gratitude the extensive discussions I have had with Yuval Cohen (on Fortunate Misfortune), Patricia Greenspan (on Not Being Sorry), Mark Sainsbury (on the nature of paradox), Alex Tabarrok (on Beneficial Retirement), Meshi Uri (on the punishment paradoxes); and with Michael Clark, G. A. Cohen, Nir Eyal, Cecile Fabre, Meir Hemmo, Kasper Lippert-Rasmussen, and Hillel Steiner on a number of the paradoxes each. Some people sent me papers replying to my paradoxes; of those, papers by James Lenman, Kasper Lippert-Rasmussen, and Tal Manor have been or are about to be published, together with my replies. I obviously appreciate the attention given to my work.

Alon Chasid, Avner de-Shalit, David Enoch, Amihud Gilead, Michael Gross, Doug Husak, Hagar Kahana-Smilansky, Menachem Kellner, Iddo Landau, James Lenman, Tal Manor, Jeff McMahan, Ariel Meirav, Avital Pilpel, Alma Smilansky, Jonathan Smilansky, Daniel Statman, Simon Wigley, and Nick Zangwill merit special gratitude for generously reading and giving me comments on all or most of the manuscript. They have made a large contribution to the book. Iddo, Hagar, and Danny deserve further commendation for having done this while having previously read almost every one of the paradoxes as an individual paper. Surely they carry a particularly large burden of responsibility for any errors that remain.

I have benefited from the opportunity to go over a draft of this book with my students at the University of Haifa, in classes during the winter of 2004 and the spring of 2006. I have given talks about some of these paradoxes to more academic forums than I can mention here, in Denmark, Israel, Portugal, Turkey, the United Kingdom, and the United States.

Three of the paradoxes were written, and the project of making this book was conceived and undertaken, during my sabbatical year at Rutgers University in 2003–4. I am thankful for the hospitality provided by the wonderful philosophy department

Acknowledgments

at Rutgers. I want to note my particular gratitude to a number of people: to Larry Temkin, for being my sponsor and a most welcoming host in the department, and for hours of philosophical conversation; to Jeff McMahan, for continuous caring and thoughtful contributions, both philosophical and non-philosophical; and to Doug Husak, for many pleasant lunches spent talking mostly about punishment. Susan Viola, Mercedes Diaz, Pauline Mitchell, and Matthew Wosniak took care of my needs in the department and helped to make that year so pleasant and productive.

I was very fortunate to have had the assistance of Alice Koller in making the manuscript clearer and better written, and I am grateful to her for her efforts and good advice. I am grateful to Anthony Grayling for his generous counsel and encouragement on publication. Nick Bellorini, the philosophy editor at Blackwell, was enthusiastic about the project from the very beginning, and has been an ideal editor since. The two reviewers for Blackwell were at once sympathetic to the nature of the book and critical in helpful detail. It was a pleasure to work with Gillian Kane, Kelvin Matthews, and Valery Rose on the design and production of the book. Alma Smilansky drew the diagrams. Marion Lupu made the final touches on the manuscript and checked the proofs.

I shall not begin to describe my gratitude to various friends who helped in ways related to this book, most of whom are mentioned here in other capacities; I am sure that they know who they are and what I feel. I must, however, make an exception for Iddo Landau, who has followed my struggles with the paradoxes and the book so closely, and has been so helpful and supportive at every stage. As always, I have been sustained in my efforts by the love of my mother, Sarah, and of Hagar, Alma, and Jonathan. To Jonathan, my brother, I dedicate this book.

I gratefully acknowledge here the permission of the editors and publishers to make use of the following articles: "Two apparent paradoxes about justice and the severity of punishment," *Southern Journal of Philosophy* 30 (1992), 123–8; "Fortunate misfortune,"

Ratio 7 (1994), 153–63; "May we stop worrying about blackmail?" *Analysis* 55 (1995), 116–20; "Preferring not to have been born," *Australasian Journal of Philosophy* 75 (1997), 241–7; "Blackmail," *Encyclopaedia of Ethics*, 2nd edn. (London: Routledge, 2001); "Choice-egalitarianism and the paradox of the baseline," *Analysis* 63 (2003), 146–51; "On not being sorry about the morally bad," *Philosophy* 80 (2005), 261–5; "The paradoxical relationship between morality and moral worth," *Metaphilosophy* 36 (2005), 490–500; "The paradox of beneficial retirement," *Ratio* 18 (2005), 332–7; and "The paradox of moral complaint," *Utilitas* 18 (2006), 284–90.

Acknowledgments

Introduction

[T]he point of philosophy is to start with something so simple as not to seem worth stating, and to end with something so paradoxical that no one will believe it.
Bertrand Russell, *The Philosophy of Logical Atomism*

If God is all-good, all-powerful, and all-knowing, then how can there be so much suffering and evil in the world? If every event, including every choice we make, has a cause (otherwise, how could it happen?), then, since the cause of that choice existed, how could we have chosen otherwise than we did choose?

Like many other people, I became interested in philosophy in my teens largely through the compelling interest of such apparent paradoxes. While most young people who succumb to the interest of philosophical puzzles overcome this seduction and go on to become pillars of their community, I seem not to have completed the transition. In fact the second perplexity (it is not, properly speaking, a paradox), which is a version of the free will problem, troubled me so much that I worked on it for over a dozen years. My book *Free Will and Illusion* (2000) was the outcome.[1] Paradoxes such as the notorious "Liar Paradox" or Zeno's paradoxes also intrigued me (for surveys of philosophical paradoxes, see, e.g., Poundstone 1990; Sainsbury 1996; Rescher 2001; Clark 2002; Olin 2003; Sorensen 2003). When I was new to philosophy, I often used to try out these paradoxes on innocent relatives and friends. But even that early in my education such paradoxes of logic, metaphysics, or knowledge were not what really seemed to matter; they were entertaining and could probably teach us something, but the only paradoxes that seemed genuinely important to me had some bearing on moral issues or on "the meaning of life."

Hence, my philosophical work has been concerned with moral paradoxes from the beginning. My view about the importance of moral paradoxes is not common among moral philosophers. While paradoxes are recognized as central in logic, metaphysics, and the theory of knowledge, and a huge literature reflects this centrality, paradoxes lack such a status within ethics. At least this is so within Western philosophy, particularly of the more careful and rigorous, analytic type dominant in the Anglo-American world. Not only are there no academic books about this topic, but, as far as I know, there is no general collection of essays under the title *Moral Paradoxes* or any similar title, nor is there any survey article on the topic, and no special journal issues are devoted to it. Yet such articles and books exist abundantly on paradoxes in other philosophical fields, just as they exist concerning so many issues that are "non-paradoxical" in ethics. A few moral paradoxes have played a role in contemporary analytic ethical thought, but awareness of the centrality of moral paradoxes as such, and concern for uncovering them, are rare.[2]

Why this is so is not clear, but it might have a lot to do with temperament. Paradoxes typically combine logical rigor, brevity, a certain type of wildness, and openness to threatening indeterminacies. Perhaps persons who are after this sort of rigor do not believe that morality is the place for it. And many philosophers who care about morality seem averse to the thought that moral problems can, or ought to be, treated pithily and with humor and irreverence. While in other philosophical fields paradoxes can be thought to be challenging and invigorating, in ethics, where human lives and social structures can be affected, it is natural to view them as paralyzing or otherwise dangerous. Also, moral paradoxes are difficult to come up with! These may be some of the reasons for the neglect of this topic, both substantively and methodologically. In my view the "pursuit of paradox" is a large part of the philosophical endeavor, even though we hope that the paradox will not be the end of inquiry; and to the extent that we believe that clear and deep thinking is morally important, such pursuit is also a moral undertaking.

Moral paradoxes are entertaining, but despite all of the fun that we can have with them, they are also aggressive threats to fundamental moral intuitions, to our ethical theories, and in general to our peace of mind. In common life when we see a small wound we try to heal it quickly, we want to bandage it over. Good philosophy does the opposite. It aims to find or even to generate wounds where everything seems obvious and well, scratching along furiously when a small wound appears. In this, as in other ways, paradoxes are the epitome of philosophy. They appear at the cutting edge of our understanding, and allow us to go deep. Paradoxes are the haikus of philosophy: troubling and humorous, short and infinite, logical and existential.

The book operates on two levels. First, by presenting ten distinct original paradoxes, each exploring a different topic, which help us to see morality and life differently. These can be read individually. Second, by gradually exploring – through the paradoxes, and in two chapters dedicated to this – what it means to say that morality and life are paradoxical, and how we should deal with this.

What is a paradox? Some philosophers are unwilling to consider certain problems to be paradoxes unless the views being explored meet the criterion of leading to strictly logical contradiction. Other people, even including some philosophers, are too permissive. They use the term "paradox" when speaking about something merely perplexing, unusual, unexpected, or ironic. The moral paradoxes that I present here show that the area between these two undesirable extremes is very broad. We shall not require strict logical contradiction, but nevertheless be quite rigorous in what we consider to be a paradox. W. V. Quine, in his classic essay "The Ways of Paradox," asks (and replies): "May we say in general, then, that a paradox is just any conclusion that at first sounds absurd but that has an argument to sustain it? In the end I think this account stands up pretty well" (Quine 1976: 1). This is, in my view, a bit too lax, for sounding absurd "at first" is not enough: a surprising but (on reflection) easily acceptable conclusion is not a paradox. R. M. Sainsbury, in his *Paradoxes*, captures the adequate strength in an elegant definition: "This is what I understand by a paradox: an apparently unacceptable conclusion derived by apparently acceptable reasoning from apparently acceptable premises" (Sainsbury 1996: 1).[3] Often, we shall see, the premises and reasoning of the paradoxes are not only apparently acceptable, but seemingly undeniable.

Quine distinguishes three kinds of paradoxes: veridical, falsidical, and paradoxes of antinomy. In veridical paradoxes a seemingly absurd result is shown to be true. We should accept its truth, and learn to see that it is not paradoxical. Falsidical paradoxes involve the defense of false results (e.g., 1 = 2; or the denial of our familiar ideas about movement in "Achilles and the Tortoise"), and can be dissolved through the rejection of a premise or an argument. In paradoxes of antinomy, two chains of argument lead to contradictory results, each of which seems to be well supported. We seemingly cannot give up on either side.[4]

In addition to those traditional terms, I think that we need another notion, that of an *existential paradox*. This type of paradox shares truth with the veridical paradox, but here the paradoxicality is real. While it seems that for Quine a veridical paradox is true and only apparently paradoxical, the existential paradox is true and really paradoxical. In an existential paradox the conclusion appears absurd even after due reflection, but it needs to be simply accepted as true in spite of its absurdity. The fault is not in the assumptions or in the argumentation that leads from them to the paradoxical conclusion, as in falsidical paradoxes, but in the "reality" this conclusion describes. Philosophers who encountered non-moral paradoxes were led, historically, by the emphasis on strict contradiction to focus on exploring what has gone wrong, namely, the premises of the argument or its validity. But as we shall see, some cases of moral paradox disclose rather that a segment of moral reality (on our best understanding of morality) is absurd. In this sense the "existential paradox" is constructive: we do not need to backtrack desperately and examine how we got to the conclusion, in order to dispose of it, but on the contrary – the paradoxical result is a revelation of how things are. There are a few parallels in the discussion of the non-moral paradoxes. Poundstone, for instance, asks "Are paradoxes 'all in our heads' or are they built into the universal structure of logic?" (Poundstone 1990: 19). Our focus will be on moral paradoxes. A paradox, then, can also be an absurd conclusion derived by acceptable reasoning from acceptable premises.

What makes for absurdity? To say that a state of affairs is absurd, in the sense that concerns us, is to say something about the fundamentally alien relationship between this state of affairs and human reason, human nature, or our basic expectations about the moral order. Beyond this broad characterization, we shall leave this notion intuitive, and assume that it will become clearer in the course of our discussion of those paradoxes where it is relevant. Since I shall aim to use the term "paradox" in a robust sense, the corresponding absurdity will need to be substantial in order for there to be a paradox.

My paradoxes will divide into all of these kinds of paradoxes. The paradoxes are certainly a mixed bunch, and each one is discussed in a different way, as seems appropriate to it.

Chapter 1, "Fortunate Misfortune," deals with a special but common situation in which it is unclear what to make of certain types of severe formative experiences. I take up cases where something very bad has happened to people (such as being born with serious physical handicaps, or into abject poverty), but then these same difficulties turned out to contribute to and greatly improve their lives, overall. This raises the question of how this initial misfortune should be viewed. Has it been a misfortune, that has been overcome, or in fact good fortune? Do the people deserve our pity and compensation for the misfortune, although it has made their lives better, overall? Paradoxically, we are inclined to think at once that these experiences were and were not misfortunes. I conclude that in many cases of FM, we should bite the bullet: even the most severe misfortune needs to be seen as good fortune, despite the lingering paradoxicality this view seems to involve.

Chapter 2, "The Paradox of Beneficial Retirement," is a rather threatening argument pertaining to many people, concerning when one ought to retire. Dealing with the seemingly familiar materials of daily life, it raises an unexpected prospect. I argue that in many professions and pursuits (such as with medical doctors or academics), perhaps 50 percent of the people ought to consider leaving their positions, if they have integrity, because people better than they are likely to replace them.

Chapter 3, "Two Paradoxes about Justice and the Severity of Punishment," brings out in an extreme way the tension that lies within our prevalent notions concerning the role that efficiency and desert ought to play in sentencing. On the one hand, most criminals from poor social backgrounds have mitigating factors in their favor due to the harsh environment in which they grew up. On the other hand, and largely for the same reasons, many of them are also likely to need the threat of more severe punishment if they are to be deterred. This means that morally curious things begin to happen, which I describe as two related paradoxes.

Chapter 4, "Blackmail: The Solution," considers the two traditional paradoxes about blackmail. The second (and more troubling one) compares cases of ordinary blackmail, such as threatening a man with disclosing his infidelity to his wife unless he pays, to many other common social practices. These seem similar but, unlike blackmail, are not thought to be so morally odious, and are not illegal. The traditional paradox then claims that ordinary blackmail is not relevantly different from those other practices. So, do we need to broaden our understanding of blackmail considerably, and forbid many common practices, or should we decriminalize ordinary blackmail? After examining the many attempts to explain what is special about blackmail, which I conclude are not successful, I offer a solution of my own. Although convincing, this solution is somewhat paradoxical itself.

Chapter 5, "The Paradox of Non-Punishment," considers a radical proposal for preventing both crime and punishment, by using the threat of harsh and disproportionate punishment to deter would-be criminals from certain types of crimes. If we achieve perfect deterrence, then there is at once no crime and no punishment, which sounds ideal. But it is dubious whether a justice system can threaten with punishment that would be unjust (even if there is no need for it to be carried out and hence no resulting injustice). This is a proposal whose rejection as well as acceptance would seem to be paradoxical.

Chapter 6, "On Not Being Sorry about the Morally Bad," explores circumstances in which it might be morally permissible not to be sorry (or even to be happy) when morally bad things happen to others. I show this through the examination of cases, ranging from innocent babies to neo-Nazis and rapists. But while the cases are intuitively convincing, how can morality say this?

Chapter 7, "Choice-Egalitarianism and the Paradox of the Baseline," is a *reductio ad absurdum* argument against the leading version of philosophical egalitarianism, a "pro-equality" position which aims to respect choice and responsibility when thinking about justice and equality. Although if one has egalitarian assumptions this version of the view initially appears to be optimal, it ends up having ridiculous implications.

Chapter 8, "Morality and Moral Worth," elucidates the conflict between the purpose of true morality (such as to eliminate suffering and grievous wrongs), and the fact that it is those same conditions that need to be eliminated that call forth the moral actions that confer moral value. Morality ends up being like one of those mythological animals that swallow their own tails.

Chapter 9, "The Paradox of Moral Complaint," takes up the relationship between what we do and what we can say about what others do to us. I consider three examples, of gossips, violent criminals, and terrorists, who want to complain about the actions of others. When can people complain? It emerges that this is not at all clear.

Chapter 10, "Preferring Not to Have Been Born," investigates the seeming impossibility of preferring not to have been born while also thinking that one's life is worth living. We see that this may make sense, which broadens our understanding of what is rational, and has relevance to our judgment of people in marginal situations (for example, people who are very sensitive, or despise themselves, or are weary of life in old age).

Chapter 11, "A Meta-Paradox: Are Paradoxes Bad?" is a meta-paradox that emerges when we return to some of the other paradoxes that have been investigated, and asks whether we should regret paradoxes and seek to prevent their occurrence. We see that the existence of paradoxes is often an indication that things are going well, morally and personally, and that sometimes paradoxicality should even be encouraged.

Chapter 12, "Reflections on Moral Paradox," is our concluding chapter. After surveying our exploration of the paradoxes, we take up a number of questions, which deal with the implications of the emerging paradoxicality of morality and human life. The results are complex and, I hope, will be thought to be interesting.

The "Postscript: The Future and Moral Paradox" looks to the future and its possible impact on moral paradoxicality.

Our discussion need not assume much beyond the minimal requirement for any philosophical argument within morality: moral conversation is an arena in which reasons are given and can be evaluated as convincing or unconvincing, and in which judgment is criticized, corrected, and broadened.

When done properly, philosophy is critical, rational, and intellectually honest. Philosophy is not a set of doctrines, and it is not so much even a body of knowledge. Rather, philosophy is primarily a process, a way of approaching certain types of problems. This means that those who are unfamiliar with philosophy cannot learn it by grasping a set of facts but only by becoming acquainted with the way in which it does its work. This book should be helpful to those who are willing to make the effort. No prior study of philosophy is required.

Very little philosophical terminology will be used in the book. The only example that will come up often is the moral theory known as "utilitarianism." Utilitarianism is the view, roughly, that one should always act so as to maximize the total sum of happiness or welfare in the world. A few other terms will be explained as they come up.

Beyond their specific significance, what does the existence of the paradoxes teach us more generally, about philosophy, morality, or life? Such questions will be taken up in the last two chapters, the meta-paradox and the concluding "Reflections on Moral Paradox," after we have become familiar with the individual paradoxes. I believe that moral paradoxes have a distinct contribution to make to our philosophical understanding of morality, and of ourselves. Paradoxes are embedded in our moral, social, and personal reality, exhibiting the richness, complexity, and occasional perversity and irrationality of life. Paradoxicality is here to stay, and we need to learn from it, and to learn to deal with it. In the future, the Postscript suggests, this will only become more so.

From all of this, the open-ended nature of the issues, and the scope for further efforts that they invite, will become apparent. I do not claim to provide exhaustive or final discussions. The book aims to open our minds, to show how analytic moral philosophy can be simultaneously enjoyable and illuminating, to pose new questions, to propose possible solutions when I have found them – and to challenge the reader to wrestle with the paradoxes him- or herself. Finally, although I have in mind some thematic or even aesthetic sense behind my ordering of the paradoxes, except for the meta-paradox (in Chapter 11), they need not be read in the sequence of my offering. As with a collection of short stories, the reader may skip and choose. For those who dare, best simply to jump in with the paradoxes.

9

NOTES

1   My work on free will has also generated paradoxes. The most surprising concern hard determinism and moral worth (Smilansky 1994a; Smilansky 2000: sec. 10.1). Some critics have indeed

asserted that my whole position on free will is paradoxical. I have not included these already published discussions in the present book: none of the ten moral paradoxes directly concerns free will.

2 An exception is Derek Parfit's early work, primarily in *Reasons and Persons* (1984), which has been an inspiration and an influence on my own. But note that, while Parfit's specific paradoxes have generated interest, his example in seeking them has not been followed. Parfit himself has turned his attention in other directions. The late Gregory Kavka also combined in his work morality and paradox (see his 1987), but sadly passed away at an early age. There has been some discussion of paradox in the political context, particularly within game theory (see, e.g., Brams 1976), although the discussions rarely focus on authority. A search for the word combination "moral paradox" in the standard philosophical data base, the "Philosopher's Index," going back 65 years all the way to 1940, yielded a mere eight results, three of them on Plato's so-called "Socratic paradoxes," and two on nuclear deterrence.

3 Roy Sorensen (2003) plausibly argues that not all paradoxes would fit this mold, but for our purposes the Quine–Sainsbury type of definition will do.

4 Doris Olin (2003) rightly notes that there are two distinctions here: one is whether there is a single line of argumentation (which she calls type 1 paradox) or two separate lines (type 2). The second distinction is about the result being veridical or falsidical. But I shall continue to use Quine's familiar terminology. A given paradox may be described as an example of different kinds of paradox (say, as a veridical paradox or as an antinomy), but one description will be more adequate.

1 Fortunate Misfortune

Mortals grow swiftly in misfortune.
Hesiod, *Works and Days*

Some people have easier lives than others, and some people have better lives than others. There is no necessary connection between these two banalities. Sometimes, however, people seem to encounter misfortune, by suffering great unchosen hardships and being confronted with severe undesired difficulties, in ways that facilitate their success and happiness in life. This creates a problem: if a seemingly unfortunate aspect of a life has proven to be beneficial overall, then it would appear not to have been a genuine misfortune. However, certain aspects of actual lives would seem to be obvious misfortunes, irrespective of whatever occurs thereafter. It thus seems open to us to assert that the life-aspects under consideration are misfortunes and also to deny that they are. Simply saying that they have been both a misfortune and not a misfortune would not do: the question which concerns us is whether something has been an unfortunate, regrettable occurrence. We shall understand this question in the "overall" or "at the end of the day" sense and, as we shall see, the difficulty does not result from ambiguity or indecision. There are here two opposing views, and we rightly seek a reply. This paradoxical state of affairs is not only interesting in itself, but also relevant to many criteria in accordance with which we evaluate our own or other people's lives, both morally and non-morally. I have certainly found that this notion helps to make sense of aspects of my own life (which is unsurprising, given that some personal experiences led me to think of the paradox).

As this is our first paradox, we shall take our time in explaining it, first setting the initial assumptions required in order for it to be a paradox, and then building up the two sides of the antinomy. This needs to be a process where, as through a sieve, irrelevant elements are extracted, until we see under which conditions the paradox exists, and the strong pull of the opposing claims that make it a paradox.

Consider the cases of Abigail and Abraham. Abigail was born with a combination of unfortunate defects: a serious breathing difficulty, and a little-known muscle disease that made it difficult for her to use her legs. Fortunately, the local doctor recommended early on that she learn how to swim and continue swimming in an intensive way. Abigail lived in a poor village far away from a swimming pool and from the sea. However, a charity in the closest city heard of her case and the doctor's advice, and it made some minimal arrangements that enabled her to travel to a swimming pool. With her parents' active encouragement, Abigail learned to swim and swam persistently. After a number of years her breathing and her ability to use her legs became normal. In the process, swimming became central to Abigail's identity, she put even more effort into it, and found it increasingly fulfilling. In time, she became an excellent swimmer, pioneered a slightly different movement of the legs for the backstroke (which was better suited to her original difficulties), and became for many years the world backstroke champion in women's swimming.

Abraham grew up in very poor surroundings. Despite being very talented, he had to leave school at an early age in order to help support his family, and he never completed his high school education. These difficulties made Abraham ambitious, and they steeled his character to an unusual degree. After years of hardship, he managed to open his own small business selling used tools. With almost superhuman hard work and painstaking attention, he built his business into a worldwide empire. Today he is one of the wealthiest people in the country, and enjoys his wealth.

The cases of Abigail and Abraham invite us to note some uncontroversial points. Things did not seem to go well for them at the beginning of their lives: if we consider only those early years, we would certainly say that in several respects Abigail and Abraham were unfortunate to an extent that many people are not. It would also be hard to deny that, whatever might have happened later in their lives, their initial suffering is in itself a bad feature of their lives. Even if we do not take account of the memories that will accompany Abigail and Abraham to the end of their lives, the pain, the shame, and the despair existed and cannot be erased. In both their lives, there were many very hard, and even bad, years, irrespective of the consequences. And it is also clear that their ultimate success was not a freak of luck: they made their separate successes in the teeth of misfortune, against the odds, and largely by themselves.

These last two elements – that the seeming misfortune involves serious harm or suffering, and that its connection with the good fortune not be artificial – help make Fortunate Misfortune into an important paradox. The first is crucial. Consider a person who breaks his leg, is taken to hospital, and ends up falling in love with the doctor, living happily ever after with her. This is less a case of Fortunate Misfortune than of a blessing in disguise. While breaking a leg is not normally good fortune, it is easy to discount the unfortunate aspect in view of the happiness that resulted from it in this case. Whatever we may think in the end about the cases of Abigail and Abraham, we cannot discount their early hardship in the same way that we do with the man's broken leg. The scale and duration of the misfortune are such that they pale in the latter case, but not in the former.

Further, in the hospital case the causality was accidental: unless this person had broken his leg, his chances of meeting that doctor would probably have been negligible, but he himself was not transformed by the accident. The more interesting cases are those in which the misfortune was inherently connected with the good fortune: the misfortune and the good fortune are non-accidentally part of the same life history. In the cases of Abraham and Abigail, the good fortune – given the prior misfortune – is *not* accidental; whereas in the hospital case the good fortune *is* accidental, even given the prior misfortune. In the cases of Abigail and Abraham we have *one* intervention of fortune, which is seemingly both bad and good; in the hospital case, by contrast, we have *two* interventions of fortune, one bad (breaking a leg), the other good (meeting the doctor). Cases such as those of Abigail and Abraham, who have been formed by the misfortune, pose the paradox in a deep way.

The interesting question concerns a successful life as a whole, and not a successful career or other mere parts of a life. But for the purpose of exposition I will speak without qualification about success, and assume that success in sport or business has given Abigail and Abraham a successful and happy life. There are plenty of other examples of Fortunate Misfortune beyond sport and business: for example, cases in which the success that depended upon the hardship is artistic; or in which the success is not even necessarily related to achievements beyond oneself, such as becoming a more reflective or a more sensitive person.

It is, I trust, becoming clear that our ordinary notions of fortune and misfortune are leading us into difficulties. For, it is very reasonable to assume that Abraham would not have reached the degree of success that he achieved had he not been "unfortunate" to begin with. And this is equally so in the case of Abigail. But assuming that Abraham and Abigail are happier at the end than they would have been had they not originally been unfortunate creates problems for us. It invites the thought that the "misfortunes" of Abigail and Abraham were actually their good fortunes.

There is a question about whether you can judge me to be better off overall although I disagree that I am better off overall. But this question need not detain us, for we assume that Abigail and Abraham would agree with the claim that they are better off overall than they most probably would have been without the original hardship. In other words, my discussion of the paradox assumes that the person's subjective perception agrees with the judgment that his or her misfortune has been beneficial. We can call this the "subjectivity condition." Another question is whether one may agree that one is better off overall as a result of some factor, but could still rationally prefer that this factor had not intervened, that is, prefer to have remained less well off. This question as well does not concern us, for we assume that Abigail and Abraham would say that they are happy to be better off.

We must not make light of such assumptions. Many cases that seem to be instances of Fortunate Misfortune cannot, under the subjectivity condition, be considered genuine. For example, some people would honestly claim to be more than willing to give up any later success "caused" by their misfortune, if they could have had a happy childhood. Or they may believe that the hardship and the success are incommensurable and cannot be weighed against each other, or that any verdict about their lives and happiness would be too ambiguous. But many other people would say that, even having suffered hardship, they have ultimately gained from it, and would not prefer living the lives they would probably have led if the misfortune had not occurred.

What then is under contention? Quite simply, Abigail and Abraham would insist that, since their childhood hardship was so substantial, and since their success has required such great effort on their part to overcome it, this hardship must be considered a misfortune. They would thus object to, and are likely even to resent, any insinuation that their hardship has not in fact been a misfortune. It is this last issue, whether Abigail and Abraham had been unfortunate in spite of their visible success in their later years (which depends on the misfortune), that concerns us.

We can imagine circumstances in which versions of our two characters, now named Abigail* and Abraham*, would have been just as successful and just as happy without the original hardship. Hardship as such is surely not necessary in order to achieve success or happiness (there *is* a sense of "success" where it consists of the overcoming of difficulties, but we are not limiting ourselves to this sense). If Abigail had not been born handicapped, if Abraham's parents had won the lottery when he was born, and if both Abigail and Abraham had been born with rare musical talents, perhaps they both would have been successful and happy without any early hardship. We can admit that this would have been preferable. But it is not clear that this makes much difference to the paradox. For the real Abigail and Abraham, hardship was in fact a *condition* for ultimate success. We need not conduct a complex investigation into the nature of the necessity. It suffices that, other things being equal, they would not have been as successful, or as happy, without the hardship.[1] How, then, can this hardship be considered their misfortune?

Think for a minute about a very different case. Take Zelda, for example. Her original "good fortune" (her doting parents, the wealth she was born into and all that it has bought for her) has "spoiled" her, diluted her ambition, her work habits, and her ability to persevere. She gets discouraged easily, and lacks the strength of character to do much with her life. It is not that she is utterly miserable, but she simply has not managed to amount to much. She also lacks any of the deeper joys and feelings of achievement that Abraham and Abigail have. Unfortunate Zelda. Perhaps she is the true victim of misfortune, not Abigail and Abraham.

It would appear that things have gone seriously awry. Perhaps our difficulties begin when we do not take full account of the fact that the Abigails and Abrahams of this world are extraordinary in having overcome odds so great that most people in similar circumstances succumb to them. It is a personal triumph for Abigail, a triumph over misfortune, that she has not let herself become a spiritless invalid, just as it is a triumph for Abraham not to have become mediocre and bitter. Anyone who denies this does not do Abraham and Abigail justice, or – worse – falls into a simplistic and extreme position on free will and determinism. Or so it can be argued.

Let us put to one side the free will problem, and try to further clarify our central difficulty. One way might be to say that Abigail and Abraham would deride any talk about Fortunate Misfortune.

Saul Smilansky

They would instead say something like the following: "Not only have we had such an unfortunate start, unfortunate both in itself and compared to that of others, but we have managed to achieve a great deal, and much more than most. Ours is a double triumph: overcoming misfortune, and achieving so much. We actually deserve pity and even compensation for having been unfortunate, as well as deserving the laurels of our later success, and particular appreciation for having won them on such hard terms."

Once Abigail and Abraham put matters in this way, however, we seem able to reply to them. In their cases the later success is not incidental to the earlier hardship: it is dependent on it. Without the early "misfortune," their characters would not have formed as they did, and their achievements, and resulting happiness, would not have materialized. And so, without denying the suffering involved in the early hardship, we cannot now consider it a "misfortune."

This however is surely outrageous. What about the pain, the fear, the humiliation, the daily demands for survival, the idea of being singled out among those more fortunate, the sense of helplessness? Am I claiming that, to live your childhood in gruelling poverty, to be denied an opportunity to learn and to develop your talents, and to have to struggle for years to eke out a minimal living, are not misfortunes? Am I denying that it is a misfortune in childhood to be unable to breathe properly and hardly able to walk, not for a short time but for many years? To deny in general that these are misfortunes would be very implausible, and cruel.

And yet, the puzzle remains. Perhaps we ought to say that such hardships would be a misfortune for most people, but for Abigail and Abraham they have not been misfortunes. Or, rather, that Abigail and Abraham have managed to turn this potential misfortune into non-misfortune, or – I hesitate – perhaps into good fortune. The meager opportunities for self-development that their early circumstances offered to Abigail and Abraham have in fact proved to be catalysts for such development. On this view, whether something is a misfortune cannot be determined in itself, even in seemingly obvious cases such as Abigail's. It

Fortunate Misfortune

depends also upon what one makes of it, what it makes of one. In short, it depends upon what happens later. Abigail and Abraham cannot claim to have suffered a misfortune for which they might be pitied or compensated if this "misfortune" is crucial in having made them what they are, what they are proud of being: successful and happy. A misfortune, on this view, can be entirely compensated and redeemed by its ultimate beneficial effects.

Is this a plausible view? The air of paradoxicality lingers, for can we really see Abraham and Abigail, with the childhoods I described, as not having suffered a misfortune? When we can say so clearly (at the time that certain terrible events occurred) that these events were misfortunes, can the evaluation "misfortune" really depend so completely on what emerges later on? Is the misfortune's status as a misfortune not secured by the fact that even if it were compensated for, there was so much that needed compensation? Who would not view such a childhood for his own children as a misfortune, whatever might happen later? Moreover, does a misfortune cease to be one merely because it is overcome through great and unusual efforts?

But then thoughts supporting the "non-misfortune" view return once more: while Abigail and Abraham have confronted an apparent misfortune, this can hardly be viewed as unfortunate for them, as a similar situation would typically be for others. Yes, they were desperately unhappy – but as a result became much happier than they otherwise would have become. Yes, they were nearly crushed by cruel forces of nature or society – but as a result became successful agents and unusually capable masters of their own destiny. We do not have to follow Dostoevsky or Nietzsche in speaking about the ennobling features of suffering, to see that Abigail and Abraham have benefited. Their lives have become better.

The pendulum of arguments and intuitions goes back and forth. It seems that one wants to insist both that such people have been, and that they have not been, unfortunate.

So, perhaps we need to acknowledge and remain with the paradoxical antinomy, which is deeper and stronger than any

Saul Smilansky

purported solution. That is a defensible position. My own view, most of the time, denies that Abigail and Abraham have suffered a misfortune. Although clearly they have suffered, this has not been a real misfortune for them. However, the idea that people like Abraham and Abigail have not been unfortunate (or that they have even been fortunate) remains paradoxical, even if true. Once we enter the land of paradox, even a solution (the correct choice in the antinomy) does not dispel all of the paradoxicality. This is perhaps a sign of a genuine paradox.

There is a further paradoxical twist here: by succeeding through great effort and sacrifice, one forfeits some of the pity and compensation that might be due to those who make no effort and end up failures: one "gives up" certain benefits by overcoming. It seems paradoxical to say that if you have overcome a misfortune then it was not in fact a misfortune, but this may well be the correct view.

Many of us have experienced hardships, probably more limited ones than those of Abigail and Abraham, from which we have benefited. What seemed to be bad fortune has often turned out to have welcome effects, making us stronger, better able to appreciate life, more mature, wiser, or more humane. If what I have been saying is convincing, we generally ought not to treat these hardships as misfortunes. It is not that one always ought to positively seek hardships that might be ultimately beneficial. But if such hardships have occurred, then, while we might in a certain case regret that the whole (hardship + success) combination had been necessary for the success, we cannot easily grudge the hardship while at the same time welcoming the effect.

One nagging thought remains. True, Abigail and Abraham's lots in life are ultimately not bad ones. But it is they who, in the face of overwhelming difficulties have made it "not bad." And they did not choose to undergo a certain amount of hardship in return for the prospect of a later success: they were thrown into the hardship, left to struggle as best they could or to drown. Do they not deserve our pity for having had to undergo all of this? Something is right here, but its rightness does not substantially change our earlier conclusion. They of course deserve sympathy for the suffering, humiliation, and fear they suffered as children. It is also a pity – it is unfortunate – that Abigail and Abraham did not have an easier but just as successful a life. But while they deserve our sympathy and appreciation for overcoming a situation of great difficulty and potential misfortune, it is not clear, in the light of the outcome of the earlier hardship, that Abigail and Abraham ought to be pitied, in the sense that people who have been unfortunate often ought to be pitied. Without the early hardship, Abigail and Abraham would have been worse off. In the end, this hardship has not been a misfortune for them.

We can leave this point with the words of the Jewish-Italian author Primo Levi, who underwent some of the horrors of Auschwitz, from the "Afterword" to his acclaimed book on his personal experiences, *If This is a Man*:

> On the contrary, onto my brief and tragic experience as a deportee has been overlaid that much longer and complex experience of writer-witness, and the sum total is clearly positive: in its totality, this past has made me richer and surer. (Levi 1987: 397–8)

Fortunate Misfortune occurs on the collective level as well as to particular individuals. The Dutch, whose proverbial national character and ingenuity are said to have benefited greatly from the encroachment of the sea, are only one example. Speaking about collective Fortunate Misfortune raises other issues, such as collective agency and responsibility. And a close examination of who in fact suffered the apparent misfortune and who in the end benefited is of course necessary if a case is to come under the heading of Fortunate Misfortune. There is nothing philosophically puzzling about one person's misfortune contributing to another's good fortune.

The experience of people growing up as members of groups that are systematically discriminated against, and of their becoming more resilient and more highly motivated as a result, is all too familiar. The notion of Fortunate Misfortune may be central when we try to make sense of such experiences. But what is the ethical relevance of the good fortune that results

Saul Smilansky

from the misfortune? In some sense, the resulting good fortune is irrelevant. Surely it matters most that racists intended the slight and the harm they inflicted, and that they created bad feelings that endure and obstacles that were unfair. This should suffice to make room for a need for victims of racism to be owed apology and perhaps compensation. The curious issue of Fortunate Misfortune does nevertheless seem pertinent here, at least in two ways. First, it makes for some "moral luck" for the racists, who, at the end of the day, have not caused harm of the sort that they wished for. (A collection of the central contributions on this issue is Statman 1993. The comparison between Fortunate Misfortune and moral luck can be fruitful, but I will not take it up here.) Second, Fortunate Misfortune quite obviously complicates our view of what constitutes being a victim.

Fortunate Misfortune on the collective level, the idea of "unfortunate good fortune" (such as Zelda's), or a detailed investigation into the role of fate, luck, choice, and effort in cases of Fortunate Misfortune, would each require a separate discussion. Similarly demanding would be an investigation into the many possible paradoxical corollaries of the paradox of Fortunate Misfortune: the way the issue of social equalization would play out, for example (should Abigail and Abraham compensate Zelda, who is much worse off?). Or, differently, attitudes such as remorse or forgiveness may well be transformed if one person's efforts to harm another actually proved to be a Fortunate Misfortune for the second person. But I shall not take up such matters here.

We all know that it is often very difficult to evaluate the significance of events either as they occur or afterwards, and in particular to evaluate their significance for a whole life. Occurrences of apparently Fortunate Misfortune are particularly extreme instances of this general theme, for in Fortunate Misfortune something has occurred that is in itself a clear and grim misfortune but it has resulted in good fortune. What are we to make of this? I have argued for a perhaps counterintuitive "solution" to the antinomy that lies at the basis of this paradox: in true instances of Fortunate Misfortune, it becomes doubtful whether the seemingly obvious misfortune can really be thought to be so. But even if one finds this solution philosophically satisfying, some of the absurdity remains. Even if we resolve the paradoxical antinomy as to whether people like Abraham and Abigail have been unfortunate by denying that they have, our result remains paradoxical.

NOTE

1 One might argue that a person cannot complain of conditions that made him what he is, if without those conditions he would not be the person that he is. You may have suffered what seems like a misfortune, but this misfortune made you what you are. Without the misfortune, you would not be around to do the complaining. This argument does not distinguish between Fortunate Misfortune and other kinds of misfortune, and does not create a problem specifically for us (see Parfit 1984). There are various difficulties with such a position, but I cannot take up this complex issue here. Clearly much Fortunate Misfortune does not fall under this topic, i.e., the misfortune is fortunate without radically changing one's identity, such that we would say that that person does not exist. We should try to think about Fortunate Misfortune while bracketing the "identity" (or "non-identity") problems. I assume here a largely unified and stable notion of the self. I also ignore, in the context of this discussion, complications arising from changes in one's judgments of preferences in the past, present, or future. Admittedly, our views might change if the misfortune comes at the end rather than the beginning of a life (see, e.g., Velleman 2000). But the Fortunate Misfortune need not, in any case, be in one's past: one might, for example, suffer from a permanent disability (such as deafness) that leads to one's becoming better off overall.

Saul Smilansky

2 The Paradox of Beneficial Retirement

A gentleman talked of retiring. "Never think of that," said Johnson. The gentleman urged, "I should then do no ill."

Johnson: "Nor no good either. Sir, it would be a civil suicide."

Samuel Johnson, quoted in Boswell's *Life of Johnson*

Morally, when should one retire from (or otherwise leave) one's job? The answer may be "now." Given that a number of conditions are met (the "Underlying Conditions"), this radical conclusion may apply to most people within many professions and pursuits. The paradoxicality appears already on the level of a single individual, but the fact that its presence seems to be so widespread increases its importance.

X is a doctor in a large hospital, Y a police detective, and Z a university professor. They are not particularly incompetent in their respective professions, but neither are they particularly good. They are, let us assume, ranked at the 80th percentile from the top (they are better than 20 percent of their peers and worse than 80 percent). Let us assume, moreover, that they are not ranked as they are because of their laziness or other factors easily within their control: even if they worked harder, they would not advance much. Over the years it has become apparent to those who work with or for them that they are not very talented or capable as doctors, detectives, or academics, although they are still above the elementary standards below which one is thrown out of the profession. Assume, finally, that the following Underlying Conditions are met:

1 There is no shortage of potential candidates for their positions.
2 New recruits in the profession are no worse, on average, than the people who have been in it for some time (or the new recruits will be considered no worse after not too long a period of adjustment).
3 X, Y, and Z can retire or find something else to do without suffering exceptional hardship (relative to the norm).
4 No unusual conditions apply (for instance, it is not the case that X, Y, and Z would be more harmful in the roles they would take up were they to leave their present positions; or that the people who would not enter the profession if X, Y, and Z stayed on would go on to do wonderful things in a different profession). And side effects will broadly even out, or be relatively unimportant, so they can be dismissed. We shall henceforth be bracketing all considerations except the potential benefit to those the profession serves.[1]

The performance of X, Y, and Z has serious negative consequences: the doctor misdiagnoses a large number of patients who otherwise could have been cured; the police detective does not catch many criminals who go on to commit serious crimes; and the academic contributes very little to the advancement of research and does a poor job of training and supervising students. We are considering cases where the work does good (bad workers in harmful jobs, who would be replaced by better workers, perhaps should not retire). We are also interested in cases where economic forces alone do not lead to optimal efficiency. Given the Underlying Conditions, if X, Y, and Z were to leave their jobs, it is very likely that others who would be better than they would replace them. In fact, statistically the chance that someone more capable would replace each of the poor performers is roughly 4:1. Hence, if these poor performers were

Saul Smilansky

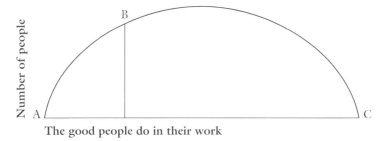

Figure 2.1 If anyone from the professionally worst group (between A and B) were replaced by someone from the whole group (between A and C), the chance that the replacement will be better is excellent.

to retire, the people they would otherwise have continued to serve would be healthier, crime would decrease, and research and professional training would improve (see Figure 2.1).

It is important to see that the argument is not based on the direct harmfulness of the relatively poor performers: they *are* productive and, for example, if X, the medical doctor, comes to work on a given day, this, taken in itself, improves matters. There would be no paradox about the moral obligation of directly harmful professionals to leave. The paradox follows only in cases that meet the Underlying Conditions, where the professional is productive, but his or her replacement is very likely to do much better.

It might seem that I am forgetting the financial costs of retirement. The strictly economic perspective would depend on many complex particulars, but typically it would point in the opposite direction: new people could be hired at lower salaries, hence actually saving money for the organization. My argument, however, is not based on financial considerations. More broadly, while the argument can be made as a proposal to revise social policy ("let us retire first the bottom 10 percent, and replace them . . ."), I am focusing here on the perspective of the individual deliberating on his or her own role. We are exploring matters not from the organizational point of view (asking, say, whether people should get tenure in their jobs), but from the point of view that focuses on the effects on others of

25

the continuing presence in that position of a given individual. A test can be devised that would help people decide whether to leave their positions. I call the test the *Existential Test*: how would things be if I were not there?

If people were to perform this test on themselves, at least half of them may reach the striking conclusion that they should retire. In certain professions there is no shortage of new applicants but, on the contrary, many people are waiting to enter (who would be, on average, similar to or better than those currently in the position); half of the people currently employed are below average, for each of them leaving their job will not cause enormous hardship (and their difficulties would be comparable to the difficulties of those newcomers who would not get good jobs unless they retire); and other effects and considerations will not be very significant. *Half of the people should each consider giving up their place for such a newcomer.*

Epistemic transparency concerning current jobholders, so that the relevant people can come to know that they are among those who should leave, is here assumed. It seems unlikely that the relevant people would not be able to realize, if called upon to think about this question, that they are not performing well, when in fact their peers would rank most of their colleagues as more competent and productive than them. Even if the poor performers are blind to the facts, those facts should be apparent to others, who can tell them. If we do not assume transparency the situation would not become less paradoxical. For then, many of the people who are well within the top 50 percent would also need to be worried about the question where they lie on this scale. It is best, I think, to assume transparency and to hold the epistemic factors constant.

I emphasize that I have been conservative here in my assumptions, in a number of ways. First, it can be claimed that potential newcomers into a profession are on average likely to be better for various reasons, such as that they will be professionally up to date, but I have not taken account of such matters. Second, I constructed the argument as though it is assumed that we do not reliably know who among those waiting to enter the profession would be better in the long run. Hence it is only the bottom 50 percent or so who need to worry, for the top 50 percent are statistically at least as likely to be replaced by someone worse than themselves, as they are to be replaced by someone better. If, as is likely, we *do* have some such pertinent probabilistic knowledge, and meritocratic hiring practices are in place, then a not very good current jobholder has an even greater assurance that someone who is better will replace him or her. This means that the "pro-retirement" argument may apply even to some of the people who are in the top 50 percent of their profession! If someone is much further down in the ranking, then assurance of an improvement, on condition of his leaving, becomes that much greater. Third, the argument is set to work independently of the similar actions of others. If, however, one has grounds for believing that one's replacement is also likely to leave in favor of a superior replacement, if it turns out in (say) a decade that he or she is below average, this would strengthen the force of the call for one to retire. Fourth, I have not given independent weight to any claims about the greater deservingness of the candidates waiting to enter the profession. The argument as formulated has focused only on the comparative good or harm that will follow to those whom the profession serves.

No doubt there would also be factors working in the opposite direction, and limiting the number of people to whom the "pro-retirement" argument might apply. In certain professions and in some circumstances these factors may have a considerable influence. But my "50 percent argument" was merely a way of emphasizing the issue, and is inevitably schematic. What matters is the paradox, and that it is likely to be relevant to a great many people.

We can understand the paradox as emerging from the contrast between the two following statements:

1 No moral problem arises as to whether a person who has acquired professional training at some personal effort, is productively employed in a socially useful task, and is working hard at it should continue working.

2   Each one among a large number of those positive, productive, hard-working people ought to leave her job.

Another way of seeing the difficulty is this: X, Y, or Z could
say that he or she wants to work because she enjoys her work,
he needs to earn the money, she wants to feel that others depend
on her, he likes to tell people what to do, and so on. However,
given the Underlying Conditions, and transparency, many (and
possibly most) people cannot sensibly and consistently make both
the following statements:

1   I am a doctor/police detective/academic because I want
people to be healthier/the streets to be safer/knowledge to
increase; and
2   I will continue working in my present job.

It might be thought that we are proceeding in the direction
of ageism, discriminating against the old in favor of the young.
This is not so much an objection to the paradox, as something
that might make it more troubling. But the logic of my argument
may well entail that a mediocre middle-aged doctor or academic
should leave his or her position so that another person, who is
approaching retirement but is much more accomplished and has
a stock of useful experience, could continue working. The argument is based on the comparative contribution of the relevant
persons, and does not necessarily depend on age factors. If many
young people were to leave their present job this might create
economic difficulties, but note that my point is not that the likes
of X, Y, and Z should not work, but only that they should not
do so in their current positions or in ones where similar conditions would apply.

It might also be claimed that the argument is depressing and
potentially harmful, and should not be proclaimed or pursued.
There is abundant empirical social-psychological evidence that
almost all people assess their own professional value more highly
than is accurate (as they also assess the way that others view them,
their driving ability, and almost every other such self-evaluative

Saul Smilansky

matter) (see, e.g., Goleman 1985; Taylor 1989). And this, as well as continued ignorance concerning the Paradox of Beneficial Retirement, should perhaps better be left as it is. Thomas Nagel has made a strong case against spelling out and exposure (1998), and I have seen reason for thinking about "positive illusions" in another context (Smilansky 2000). Such questions are not, however, our concern here. In the present case there would be both benefits and drawbacks to awareness, and we shall not attempt to evaluate the balance. We have here a paradoxical philosophical claim, and even if it were thought that it would sometimes be better to keep quiet about it, this would not affect the truth or falsity of the claim.

Finally, it might be thought that my claim is too morally demanding. Why should our doctor, detective, and academic give up their entrenched positions while the 20 percent of their colleagues who are even worse than they remain in their jobs? Moreover, have such people not trained for years and invested their efforts and hopes in getting to where they are, so that they cannot be expected to give all of this up? In other circumstances, after all, we do not usually demand such sacrifices. Note also that the "pro-retirement" argument makes everyone a potential hostage of the decisions of others, and of other such events. An interesting example of this occurred in Israel in the 1990s. Once Jews were permitted to leave the Soviet Union in large numbers, over a million immigrated to Israel within a few years, adding nearly 20 percent to the population. Among the new emigrants were a disproportionably large number of medical doctors, engineers, and other such professional people. Were the longstanding citizens automatically required to consider giving up their positions, just because of these new potential candidates for their jobs?

The question whether, all things considered, people such as our doctor, detective, or academic ought to leave their positions is complicated, and we cannot settle it here. We would need, for one, to decide how weighty moral considerations are as compared to people's desires and interests. We would also need to consider the "retirement question" from various normative-theoretical perspectives. If X, Y, and Z are act-utilitarians (a position that seeks to maximize overall happiness, but holds that this should be evaluated concerning each act in itself), matters are simple, and they obviously must leave their jobs, for doing so would increase overall utility. A robust ethical approach focusing on virtues might also mandate such a move: professional virtue would seem to require that one critically evaluate one's professional achievements, and think above all about the victims of one's decision to stay on nevertheless (dead patients or crime victims, for instance). Certain interpretations of a morality of commands and constraints (deontology), or of ways of thinking about morality as a contract among people, would also be sympathetic to the radical conclusion, even if this conclusion is admittedly demanding.

It is important to notice that mine is not yet another typical utilitarian demand to do more good in the world, say, to contribute large sums of money or engage in volunteer work. The Paradox of Beneficial Retirement takes up non-utilitarian themes such as concern for one's *integrity* and the ability of making sense of one's life project (for example, as a person concerned with people's health, safety, or education). This paradox also goes beyond the idea of doing good, in that it shows that, for many well-meaning and hard-working people, their continued occupancy of their position is *harmful*. And that is a very different sort of claim. The way the notion of integrity operates in this context is particularly interesting. This notion is the mainstay of Bernard Williams's famous critique of utilitarian ways of thinking (1973b), blunting the force of the demand that people sacrifice for the common good. The importance of one's own life projects, and the sanctity of personal integrity, are used by Williams to limit people's obligations. In my argument, by contrast, similar ideas ground the very demanding call for unwanted early retirement.

As one well-respected surgeon says:

> The hardest question for anyone who takes responsibility for
> what he or she does is, What if I turn out to be average? If we

took all the surgeons at my level of experience, compared our results, and found that I am one of the worst, the answer would be easy: I'd turn in my scalpel. But what if I were a C? Working as I do in a city that's mobbed with surgeons, how could I justify putting patients under the knife? (Gawande 2004)

My aim here has not been to settle the moral question, but to pose the Paradox of Beneficial Retirement as a puzzling, important matter that needs to be thought about, at least philosophically. Such thought may take diverse forms when applied to the real lives of persons, and ought not to be limited to the "retire" or "stay on" options. If a person is roughly average professionally, then he or she will have a reason to work harder to pass beyond that threshold. The person eliminates the likelihood that his or her continuing occupation of this position thereby makes matters worse. If one is irredeemably within the scope of the argument, then remaining in one's profession but voluntarily transferring to an undesirable location, for example, might have a similar saving effect. A decision to retire "soon," or "when my economic condition improves a bit," would also often be a partial but reasonable response to the problem.

A further twist follows from the incentive that the Paradox of Beneficial Retirement would seem to provide in choosing one's career in the first place: the incentive to avoid the sort of personal and moral risk that we have been discussing. If, for instance, one opts for a line of work where it does not matter much what one does, then one would not need to worry whether one is doing harm by not giving way to a potential replacement who is better than one.

Whatever decisions such people as I have been considering make about abandoning their career, there is likely to be something sad about the result. If I am correct, a great many people have a substantial moral and personal reason to retire, even if it were thought too morally demanding to expect them to do so. To put it bluntly: for a great many people, the best professional action that they can currently take is to leave their profession.

NOTE

1   I have strengthened the specification of these conditions as a result of James Lenman's (2007) criticism of my original (2003) paper. Lenman claims that my argument is vulnerable because of the role of factors beyond the direct comparative contributions of the would-be retirees and would-be replacements, such as the lesser contribution of the retirees after they retire. But I do not think that these factors make a big difference, when compared to the benefits (such as saved lives). Lenman also argues that those among the current pool of candidates who will not get positions unless the people I discuss retire are not likely to be as good as even the worst among those who currently hold positions. They are in fact, he claims, similar to the "unsuccessful," those who did not get jobs when the current jobholders did. In Smilansky (2007) I reply showing how a variety of factors (the opening up of professional jobs to women and minorities, or the fact that many people cease being productive during their career for unpredictable reasons) undercut Lenman's argument. If underachievers retire or otherwise leave, this will help the best candidates get earlier and better positions, and give more people a chance to prove their worth. The profession and those who benefit from it will gain considerably.

Saul Smilansky

3 Two Paradoxes about Justice and the Severity of Punishment

[P]erfection is finally attained not when there is no longer anything to add, but when there is no longer anything to take away.

Antoine de Saint Exupéry, *Wind, Sand and Stars*

There is wide disagreement about the correct theory for justifying punishment. However, widespread and deep intuitions about the basic content of any satisfactory theory for justifying punishment, if such is possible, together with some plausible empirical assumptions, seem to yield two closely related paradoxes about justice and the severity of punishment. Since we share the intuitions and accept the empirical assumptions, we should be perplexed, and troubled, by these paradoxes. This pair of paradoxes resulted from my thinking about people who grew up in challenging environments.

Let us make only commonsense assumptions about punishment. We assume first of all that one central purpose of a system of punishment is deterrence. Second, we assume that some people can deserve less severe punishment for the same crime than others, and that just punishment needs to be sensitive to people's differing deserts. My arguments do not require strong assumptions about positive desert, in the sense that it is good in itself if wrongdoers suffer, but only the weaker sort of mitigating considerations of desert, which require that some wrongdoers' sentences be reduced. Since we are assuming that considerations both of deterrence (that is, the hoped-for consequences of punishment) and of desert (independent of the punishment's ability to deter further crimes) have a role to play in any adequate system of punishment, it is clear that holders of "monistic" positions will disagree: a non-compromising utilitarian is concerned only with the consequences of punishment, while a non-compromising retributivist is concerned only with exacting retribution on criminals irrespective of consequences. But there is little reason to accept these extreme positions, and most people, at least in the West, do not.

Let us now bring two empirical assumptions to bear on the discussion. First, punishment can deter, and is a reasonably effective way of deterring persons from crime. A major aim of the criminal justice system is to deter people from engaging in criminal pursuits from the start and, if this fails, to limit the return to crime (recidivism). Second, for most types of crime, the deterrent effect of punishment will generally vary among people in ways that reflect their differing socioeconomic positions. The second assumption involves the idea, roughly, that people from a lower socioeconomic background and position (the "underprivileged") will be more tempted by crime than are others (the "privileged"), and will be less apprehensive about being punished at a given level. Factors, such as their being poorer or knowing people who have crossed the line into the criminal life, may make it tempting and psychologically easier for the underprivileged to turn to crime. Hence, other things being equal, deterring the underprivileged will require a worse prospect in terms of the severity of punishment than deterring the privileged.

The notion of the "severity of punishment" can be interpreted as involving either the amount of imposition (for example, number of years in prison) or the amount of disutility generated (for example, how miserable a given prison term would make someone). In order not to burden the discussion unnecessarily, I stipulate that there is no significant difference between the privileged and the underprivileged in terms of the amount of disutility (thought to be) generated by any given level of imposition.

Saul Smilansky

We are thus able to make direct comparisons in the severity of punishments in terms of years in prison.

I shall begin by presenting a broad outline of the first paradox, modifying and explaining it, and then proceed to present the second paradox.

The First Paradox

The underprivileged usually *deserve* less severe punishment than the privileged for a given crime, other things being equal (the basis for this claim will be explored below). However, the underprivileged will usually require the *prospect* of more severe punishment in order to be deterred, other things being equal. The first formulation of the paradox, then, is this: *Justice will, by and large, require that we hand out less severe punishment to those who can be deterred only by more severe punishment.* And, broadly, the factors that necessitate more severe punishment of the underprivileged (the experiences that have hardened them to deterrence) are the very factors that make them less deserving of the punishment.

There are two ways of understanding this paradox. We can see it as coming about because justice in a narrow sense (which mitigates punishment because of lesser desert) is contrasted with the central external rationale of a system of punishment (that is, deterrence). Alternatively, we can see the paradox as internal to the notion of justice, which is understood in a broader sense: in addition to the concern with desert, justice in the broad sense itself also requires efficient deterrence. I shall proceed with the interpretation that understands justice in this context in a narrow way, as roughly equivalent to the mitigation of punishment due to lower desert.

The first paradox yields a corollary: *A just society will provide a more tempting prospect to commit further crimes for those who require a less tempting prospect in order to be deterred from committing them.*

To some extent, an even stronger formulation of the paradox is possible. We might say that, in terms of the severity of

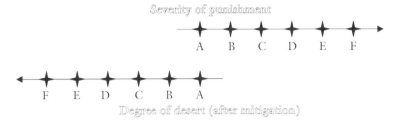

Figure 3.1 The first paradox: A, B, C, and so on indicate different people; the disparity between people's positions on the two parallel lines (the required severity of punishment and deserved mitigation) is striking.

punishment: *One's level of desert (when committing a crime) would be the inverse of the level at which one would need to be threatened with punishment in order to deter one from committing the crime.* Our subject matter, however, does not allow for such "Newtonian laws": individual levels of "deterrence-requiring" and desert are likely to differ from this general pattern, and, furthermore, punishment is only rarely individually tailored in terms of deterrence. Our discussion is inherently schematic. We shall have to speak in more general terms about the "privileged" and the "underprivileged," although some gradation in the level of the deterrence required, and in desert, is certainly possible. Yet as a broad generalization (rather than a scientific law applying to all cases) even this stronger formulation seems to be correct (see Figure 3.1).

Incidentally, a similar argument can probably be formulated in terms of individual differences in the strength of dispositions to commit certain types of crime (such as sexual ones), rather than in terms of the differences in socioeconomic background. But I shall not develop this direction here.

The commonsense attitude towards justice and punishment thus leads to this first paradox about the severity of punishment. But how are we to understand the requirement of justice that persons from underprivileged socioeconomic backgrounds ought generally to get less severe punishment for a given crime? Two general ways of spelling out our intuitions about this complex matter seem available. One focuses on what the underprivileged

Saul Smilansky

have "received from society." If some of the underprivileged have had a childhood full of psychological abuse and economic hardship, they might be said to have "paid" already (in some sense) for whatever crimes they committed. They enter a sentencing situation with a sackful of misery on their backs, and thus they do not deserve the severity of treatment that those who have had reasonably satisfying childhoods and lived under reasonable material conditions deserve (see, e.g., Klein 1990: 82–4). The second, more usual, way of understanding this issue is to focus on the criminal who comes from an underprivileged background and to point out how much greater the difficulty has been for that person to abstain from crime. If he has consistently faced strong temptations to commit crimes that the privileged have faced only in a very moderate way (if at all), as a result of influences in his past, role models in his present life, and the disparity between his poverty and the surrounding wealth, it does not seem fair if this factor is not taken into account.

The inclination of the law towards equal sentencing might seem to endanger my case here, which is based on mitigating punishments because of lesser desert (and the disparity between the reduced sentences and those needed for deterrence). Legal systems do tend to desire equal sentencing for a given crime so that the predictability of the "price per offense" will be widely known, and to avoid abuses, among other reasons. However, other tendencies within the law favor my case: legal systems also tend to leave room for other considerations beyond that of equal sentencing. And this we clearly want them to do. The paradoxicality that we are considering will in practice depend on the extent to which legal systems do so. Note, moreover, that even equal sentencing will not eliminate all of the paradoxicality, given that the underprivileged deserve less (rather than equal) punishment.

A more serious objection would argue from the basic plurality of values involved in the idea of just punishment. Just as a good car is a reasonable compromise between various requirements (weight, safety, speed, and so on), so, it might be argued, there is nothing paradoxical about the need to balance deterrence and desert. After all, we already know that considerations of efficient punishment may contrast with those of desert in the issue of the "punishment" of the innocent (it is often thought that this problem arises only in artificial, contrived situations, but as I showed in Smilansky 1990, this is not so). Thus there seems to be nothing special about the present tension between considerations of mitigating desert and of deterrence. This, however, is a misleading interpretation of the situation in which we find ourselves in the context of punishing the underprivileged. While perfection may be unattainable, it is commonly thought that deterrence and desert can go at least a long way together. But the first paradox shows that this typically is not so. A much darker analogy is required. Imagine a world in which whenever one loved someone, that person did not love one, and vice versa. Or, dynamically, that the more one person loved another, the less that second person loved the first. Clearly, the ideal of reciprocal love would then not be met. Such a situation would be absurd, and tragic.

The Second Paradox

The second paradox follows from the same assumptions that generated the first, with one addition: that punishment is *pro tanto* a bad thing, since it involves hurting people, and thus we ought to try to minimize it. Many people share this vague general assumption, although it probably does not have such widespread support as our original assumptions. This assumption will be particularly attractive for those who think that the major justification of punishment is its good effects (primarily deterrence), and are suspicious of punishing because of desert.

We have seen that our commonsense view of justice requires us to create proportionality in the severity of punishment for a given crime, in a way that will reflect the lower deserts of the underprivileged. In the light of the other common requirement for deterrence, however, there will also be a need to punish to a certain extent (say, P) those underprivileged persons who are convicted

P + x: Actual punishment level of the *privileged* (to establish the comparative gap with the underprivileged)

P: Actual punishment level of the *underprivileged* (required for their deterrence)

P − y: Possible punishment level of the *privileged* (sufficient for their deterrence)

Figure 3.2   The second paradox: some possible levels of punishment.

of committing crimes. The requirement for proportionality will then mean that those coming from more privileged backgrounds will be more severely punished (P + x), instead of being less severely punished (P − y), as they would have been if the general needs of deterrence alone had been considered. But then, there will be a great deal more punishment for those from more bountiful backgrounds who are convicted of the crimes they commit. The need to punish the underprivileged less than the privileged should not make much difference to the severity of punishment that the underprivileged will receive, given their greater need for deterrence (we can assume that they will be punished to the minimal degree). But it will cause us to punish those from more bountiful backgrounds "unnecessarily" severely ("unnecessary" to the degree x + y) (see Fig. 3.2). But this contradicts the "additional assumption" that punishment is to be limited as far as possible, namely, if we could deter to a reasonable degree without it.

What starts out as the thought that the underprivileged ought to be punished less because of mitigating factors pertinent in their case, when coupled with the need to punish the underprivileged to the required deterrent level (P), yields a paradoxical outcome of "overpunishment" of the privileged. No one, including the underprivileged, benefits, yet the privileged are severely punished.

This is similar to the story about the customer who enters a shop with a "50% OFF FOR OLD CUSTOMERS" sign in the window, but finds that the price he is being charged is exactly the same as it had been in the past. "True," says the shop owner, in response to his protests, "but I charge new customers twice as much."

It might seem that no additional punishment of the privileged will occur, because if the privileged would be deterred by the prospect of less severe punishment $(P - y)$, then the prospect of being more severely punished $(P + x)$ would surely suffice to deter them. However, to argue in this way is to forget that levels of punishment tend to have a generality that almost never covers all individual cases. A convicted criminal from a privileged background would be given a sentence more severe than the one he would receive if the ordinary considerations applied, that is, if his sentence would deter most people from privileged backgrounds (or, for that matter, even from underprivileged backgrounds). Perhaps a few more people from privileged backgrounds would indeed be deterred by the increased severity of punishment, but presumably the level of punishment that would be adequate from the perspective of deterrence for most of those from such backgrounds is much lower (i.e., $P - y$). Those from privileged backgrounds who do commit crimes and are convicted will be punished with an "unnecessary" severity only because the proportionality of desert requires that the severity of punishment of those from such backgrounds is to be more than the relevant level for those from underprivileged backgrounds.

Note that the paradoxes follow within "ideal theory," from our doing what we ought to do, and not from error, or from non-compliance with moral requirements. Given commonsense empirical and normative assumptions and, of course, people who commit crimes, then, it is precisely when we aim to do what we should (such as mitigate the punishment of those deserving mitigation) that we fall into paradox.

Since diverse elements enter the equation of punishment, given our assumptions, it is not surprising that complexity and the need for compromise emerge. What is surprising, however, is that deterrence and desert go in opposite directions so forcefully and throughout: hence, roughly, *the more one needs to be punished the less one deserves to be* (in the first paradox). This is absurd, and remains absurd however long we contemplate it. Namely, we cannot give up the premises, nor, it seems, have we made an error of argumentation. We have to live with this absurdity. In the light of this absurdity and of its importance, an "existential paradox" emerges. This situation, in turn, yields an absurd "overpunishment" that serves no one (in the second paradox).

Finally, what does all this imply about the possibility of having an effective and just system of punishment? We cannot reach definite conclusions, because in order to do so further questions need to be addressed, primarily questions that deal with the justification and nature of desert that go beyond mitigation. But our results encourage skepticism. Once we see how thoroughly the punishment of the underprivileged is made problematic by the first paradox – by the fact that, roughly, the more an underprivileged person needs to be threatened with punishment, the less he deserves such punishment – we have a choice. We can take seriously the weight of the ideas of lower desert and mitigation, in which case we shall be greatly hindered in our attempt to make the system of punishment effective. Alternatively, we can insist on deterrence, and punish the underprivileged to the required degree (P, above). In that case we will have turned the idea of a mitigating desert into a merely formal notion: *any* socially beneficial deterrence level, however high, becomes acceptable, as long as there is a variance between the way the privileged and underprivileged are punished. Taking this second direction will also create, as a byproduct, the second paradox: the privileged will be punished even more severely only so that the punishment level of the underprivileged will look light *in comparison*.

These two paradoxes are disturbing, but I see no simple way of overcoming them. Even after realizing the paradoxicality, it is very difficult to abandon the intuitions or to reject the assumptions from which the paradoxes follow.

Justice and the Severity of Punishment

4 Blackmail: The Solution

> *I have thought that the predominance in the minds of moralists of a desire to edify has impeded the real progress of ethical science: and that this would be benefited by an application to it of the same disinterested curiosity to which we chiefly owe the great discoveries of physics.*
>
> Henry Sidgwick, *The Methods of Ethics*

The topic of blackmail brings up central topics in novel ways: the permissibility of threats and offers, the relations between morality and the law, the role of concern for consequences and for non-consequentialist ethical considerations, and the limits of freedom. The paradoxicality of blackmail has been recognized for a long time, and unlike the other essays this one does not offer a new paradox. It aims to offer a solution. "With a solution like this, who needs problems?" it might be thought, as the solution is itself paradoxical. But first we need to understand what blackmail is, and what its paradoxes are.

The notion of blackmail is sometimes applied loosely, its users merely relying rhetorically on its strong pejorative implication. I shall here consider it in a narrower and more exact sense which includes the following features: (a) a declaration of intention to act (or to refrain from acting) in a way concerning which one has no obligations, that is otherwise legally permissible, and that the blackmailer believes his or her target would find unwelcome;

Saul Smilansky

and (b) an accompanying offer not to carry out the intention on condition of the blackmailer's receiving compensation that is otherwise legally permissible. Let us call this "ordinary blackmail."

The paradigmatic example is Q's threatening to tell Z's wife about Z's involvement with another woman, unless Z pays him a large sum of money. It is legal to ask for money, and likewise it is legal to tell (or even to threaten to tell) another person's wife about her husband's infidelity. The ethical issues here are less clear. Note only that none of the separate components of "ordinary blackmail" is normally thought to be morally odious in a way that can account for the common attitude towards blackmail. Something strange is going on here.

Blackmail differs from "extortion," a coercive request accompanied by a threat to perform an *illegal* action (for example, to use violence against someone). Blackmail is also distinct from the threat to spread damaging *false* information, which might involve the idea of "defamation." "Ordinary blackmail" excludes cases in which the blackmailer's advantage comes about illicitly (say, through wire-tapping). Requests by blackmailers to be paid in unacceptable "currency" (for example, that the person being blackmailed perform an immoral or illegal act) also lie outside of blackmail in the sense that concerns us. These different cases bring up various other issues that would hamper our effort to consider the difficulties inherent in "ordinary blackmail." We want to think about the pure case.

Finally, the narrow notion of blackmail that we are considering is not limited to threatening with information (as in Q's blackmailing Z). If, for example, you asked all shops of a certain kind to pay you a monthly sum for not carrying out the credible threat of opening a competing shop nearby, thereby running them out of business, problems may arise that fall within our area of concern (see Smilansky 1995a). In fact, there is reason for thinking that this may in fact be worse, in one respect, than ordinary blackmail, since here the victim is entirely innocent, whereas in ordinary blackmail the victim has often done something wrong or at least shameful, so that he has a weaker claim to immunity. But we shall focus on the ordinary cases.

Blackmail: The Solution

The idea of "ordinary blackmail" gives rise to two apparent paradoxes, one of which is conceptual, the other substantive.

The Conceptual Paradox of Blackmail

If each of the components of the common sort of blackmail (the asking for payment, the threat to do what one is otherwise permitted to do, and the carrying out – or not – of the threat) is in itself permissible, what is the source of our powerful objection to blackmail? Why do these innocuous things become so bad when brought together? Understanding common attitudes towards extortion presents no similar difficulties for, if one is not allowed to inflict violence on others, then one is not allowed to threaten to do so, let alone to demand payment for desisting. The contrast between blackmail and extortion thus also helps to highlight the question that surrounds the negative attitude towards blackmail.

Michael Clark (1994) has countered that the request for money in "ordinary blackmail" is *backed up* by a threat, that this combination brings forth something new, and that that new thing is what's problematic about blackmail. Thus there is nothing paradoxical about the fact that, in themselves, the elements that make up the practice of blackmail are permissible. And indeed there are other similar practices (bigamy or prostitution come to mind) that are morally problematic although their components are not. The ethical significance of combined acts may hence transcend the significance of their individual elements. If, then, the first paradox is taken as formal, we can dismiss it. By pointing this out, Clark might be said to have solved the conceptual paradox.

However, the *way* in which the "alchemy" of the novel emergence of badness or wrongness operates in "ordinary blackmail" remains mysterious, and separately noting the innocuous nature of each of the elements of "ordinary blackmail" helps to bring this out. If one may threaten to do what one is (otherwise) allowed to do, offering *not* to so act in return for monetary compensation does not seem capable of bringing forth the sense of radical and novel heinousness that blackmail arouses. Our dissatisfaction with any quick dismissal of the paradoxicality of blackmail increases when we reflect on other factors. The person being blackmailed, Z, would in fact often prefer to be offered the option of paying the blackmailer, and would often take up the option if it was offered. In and of itself, Z would not welcome allowing the would-be blackmailer to sell news of the affair to the press. But since selling news is permissible, Z would wish to allow the blackmailer to sell his or her silence to Z as well. Such concerns are substantive, and they point us in the direction of the second paradox.

The Substantive Paradox

The main philosophical difficulty with blackmail follows from the apparent similarity between typical cases of "ordinary blackmail" such as Q's blackmailing Z, and common practices in social and economic life that morality does not take to be extremely reprehensible and that the law does not prohibit. In what follows I will call them the "Other Social Practices." In many labor disputes, for example, workers legally threaten to cease work in order to gain higher salaries. Employers similarly threaten to close down operations or to hire other workers if their demands are not accepted. In divorce cases each partner can threaten to prolong the proceedings if the settlement does not go his or her way. Boycotts of goods or services may be threatened in order to back up various sorts of demands. Victims of inadequately tested products may threaten to sue companies under tort law, thereby bringing adverse publicity to the producers, unless compensation is forthcoming. Politicians indirectly threaten to cut funds for groups who do not support them. Many instances of raising prices of scarce goods or services are in effect monetary demands backed up by threats. All of these common practices contain the same two features I distinguished for "ordinary blackmail." Why, then, do we consider them to be fundamentally different from blackmail when we take up a moral point of view?

One way of approaching the philosophical difficulty of blackmail is to assume that common intuitions are correct. Under this interpretation the puzzle becomes merely one of *how* to justify the status quo. Even then we still have our philosophical work cut out. A true philosophical attitude, however, will question more deeply whether common intuitions are justified at all. One of the effects of thinking about the Substantive Paradox is that we call into question basic assumptions about rights and about moral limits. The consequences of the Substantive Paradox threaten to spread in both directions. We may come to feel that we need to take a more tolerant moral stance towards "ordinary blackmail," perhaps by decriminalizing it (see Mack 1982). Alternatively, we may see the common practices that resemble blackmail as being morally equivalent to blackmail, and therefore less tolerable morally and legally. In either case, the prospect is disconcerting.

Several attempts to solve the Substantive Paradox have appeared in the literature. First, we can explain common attitudes cynically. One such explanation is that being blackmailed in the ordinary ways is frightening only to the rich and powerful, while threats from employers or politicians would rarely concern them. That people with money and power take "ordinary blackmail" but not the Other Social Practices seriously is therefore hardly surprising. But the cynical sort of explanation does not seem to explain the strength of the common attitude toward "ordinary blackmail," let alone justify it. If you learned that your brother or sister was seriously dating a person who had been engaged in "ordinary blackmail," you would be upset. This doesn't seem to be explained as a result of your being in the grip of "false consciousness" induced by the manipulations of the rich.

Second, we may concede that, in moral terms, the similarity between "ordinary blackmail" and the social practices is great, but we may still believe that the distinction commonly made between them is *legally* justified. This tack would explain away the paradox. For example, difficulties with enforcement may justify why legal attitudes towards the Other Social Practices and "ordinary blackmail" should be different, although there may be no deep moral differences between them (see, e.g., Feinberg 1988; Gorr 1992).

This approach is problematic. Although the issue of blackmail involves both moral and legal matters, we can confine the case for the existence of a paradox to the moral side. Even if society didn't legally sanction blackmail, it would be hard to deny that we hold blackmailers to be morally despicable. We don't usually express such a severe negative attitude toward those who engage in sharp economic bargaining. Even our strictly ethical intuitions tolerate practices that, on closer inspection, may seem difficult to distinguish from "ordinary blackmail." So the moral/legal divide is not a solution to the moral paradox. Moreover, we would pay a high price if we argued for a firm distinction between the moral and the legal issues. A huge gap between the two, in a context such as this, would in itself be a surprising and disturbing result. Finally, the moral and the legal seem particularly intertwined in the matter of blackmail: ethical disapproval is a central reason that our laws circumscribe blackmail.

47

A third way in which philosophers and jurists have tried to deal with the Substantive Paradox is by seeking to identify a feature of "ordinary blackmail" that distinguishes it ethically from those acceptable social practices that seem so similar. This route is the most alluring, because it would defuse the Substantive Paradox: once we look closely, "ordinary blackmail" and the Other Social Practices turn out to be substantially different. However, such a litmus test has not proved easy to formulate. Among other candidates philosophers and legal thinkers have considered coerced versus uncoerced choices, the invasion of privacy, the rights of third parties, the exploitation of an opponent's weaknesses, and the distinction between harming and not benefiting (see, e.g., Murphy 1980; Lindgren 1984; Fletcher 1993). The specific discussions are complex and intriguing, but they have not been manifestly successful. The suggestions offered seem to succeed only in limited types of cases, or to beg the question by making crucial moral assumptions as to what is morally

Blackmail: The Solution

disallowed – assumptions that the issue of blackmail shows to be contentious. For example, the "gutter press" may invade a person's privacy and exploit her weaknesses in order to make money just as a blackmailer does. A neighbor may threaten to put up that second story he has permission to build, thereby blocking one's view, unless one gives way on some land dispute. This would seem to be an instance of coerced choice and of the threat of outright harm. Yet few of us view such practices in the same way as we view "ordinary blackmail."

None of the above ways seem to succeed in resolving the Substantive Paradox. We have a strong intuition that blackmail is no ordinary matter, but a particularly loathsome pursuit, morally odious to a high degree and deserving of severe criminal and social sanction. Yet no one has so far been able to point out anything special about blackmail that justifies these intuitions.

Something else seems to be going on here that provides a "solution." But this solution itself is paradoxical. We don't single out "ordinary blackmail" because its bad features are unique but because *there is nothing good about it to overcome the badness.* My conclusion is that at the end of the day, "ordinary blackmail" and the practices I have discussed may not inherently be very different ethically. There may merely be further reasons for allowing the other practices to continue. Our intuitive sense – that something unique must be present in blackmail, to make it so manifestly vile – is a mistake. Unless we find a different explanation of the status of blackmail, we need to live with this "deflationary" conclusion, namely, that there is nothing especially negative about blackmail.

Approaches from the standpoint of rights-oriented, contractual, and virtue-based ethics may all be able to contribute here, but utilitarianism (or more broadly consequentialism, a concern for consequences not necessarily related to utility) seems to acquire a particular authority in justifying the common practices. The nastiness of using information might actually be increased when such information appears in the gutter press, but other good reasons for maintaining a free press outweigh this. Using "quasi-blackmail" to threaten and to offer advantages in economic bargaining may likewise be justified because of its economic efficiency or by virtue of the importance of the right both to offer and to withhold one's labor or employment to others. But "ordinary blackmail" offers no equivalent saving graces.

Decriminalizing "ordinary blackmail" would cause widespread social harm. Some good might emerge (certain people may refrain from wrongdoing because of the additional risk of being blackmailed), but this would be negligible as compared to the damage. The opening up of this new business opportunity, with the disappearance or decline of the major current disincentives for blackmail (the legal and moral sanctions), would mean that, overall, people would be likely to face much more blackmail. Although one may prefer to be able to buy off one's blackmailer if such a blackmailer were to exist, overall it would be better to have as few blackmailers as possible. As invasion into one's private sphere becomes commercially viable, fear for individual privacy would intensify. This would not be limited to public figures, but potentially threaten everyone. And it would typically be repetitive (that is, one would need to buy silence again and again, perhaps from more than one source, and with no guarantee that the matter would be favorably concluded). An atmosphere would prevail in which each person, no matter how intimate or how foreign, could constitute a potential enemy: Hobbes's "war of all against all." And all to what purpose?

"Ordinary blackmail" *is* coercive, hurtful, demeaning, exploitative, parasitical, and invasive, as are many other social practices. There is nothing especially bad about it. Paradoxically, what singles it out is that little or no good derives from it.

Blackmail: The Solution

5 The Paradox of Non-Punishment

Care should be taken that the punishment does not exceed the guilt.

Cicero, *De Officiis*

In the earlier essay that considered punishment (in Chapter 3), we saw how two related paradoxes emerged from our common moral and empirical assumptions. After an intermission in which we dealt with blackmail, we can return to punishment. The present paradox emerges if we begin to think "outside of the box," more openly and radically.

A situation in which a system of justice broadly like our own achieves complete deterrence seems close to ideal. In such a system no crimes are committed and, as a result, no one is punished. Some people who think about systems of justice worry mostly about crime (and other illegal activities that I'll henceforth refer to under the blanket heading "crime"). Others worry a great deal about the severe punishment meted out to human beings, even if they are guilty. And nearly everyone is worried about the "punishment" of the innocent. If we could make all these different worries subside, because our world were one in which no crimes were committed and hence no one would be punished, this would surely be wonderful.

But things are not so simple. Assume that we have a very high level of certainty about the level of threatened punishment that is necessary in order to deter crime. The likelihood that criminals will be caught is also a crucial factor in deterrence, and hence in determining the level of crime, but let us bracket this matter. Our certainty that a certain level of threatened punishment would do the job need not (and is unlikely to) apply to all crimes, but the argument can go forth even if we limit punishment to only certain sorts of crimes, or confine it to a certain range of target populations. Let us call the level of such perfect deterrence "the deterrence point."

If the deterrence point applies to crime X, so that anyone committing crime X will face punishment at the level of the deterrence point (or higher), then we can predict that no crimes of that sort will occur. Let us call this the Ideal of Perfect Deterrence. In other words, *for every potential crime X, a punishment level that reaches the deterrence point prevents both crime and punishment.* The only catch is that the deterrence point needs to be very high: it will be disproportionate to the crime, and it will often in itself be unusually severe according to commonsense standards of punishment.

In order to explain what I have in mind, I can begin by telling the story of what led to the discovery of this paradox. In retrospect I can see that a number of things did so, but the final insight is due to the London traffic authorities. While in Israel, where I live, a simple parking violation will at most generate a modest fine, with severe measures (such as towing) being reserved for proportionately serious offenses (blocking traffic, for example), in London, I was warned during a recent visit, the enforcers are merciless, and one's car is liable to be towed for any offense. This caused an immediate improvement in my parking behavior, and concentrated my mind.

Now we need only to go further in the same direction. Assume, for instance, that we want to prevent parking around a certain main public square because the public would greatly benefit if the area were free of cars. If, instead of a modest fine, the penalty were to rise to a fine of $10,000, and perhaps also include confiscating the vehicle, and if the city were to publicize these disproportionate consequences adequately, then such a heavy penalty could predictably prevent *any* instance of parking in the given area. The fine might also be pegged to one's income, as it apparently is in Finland for certain offenses, so that even the super-rich would not be tempted, since they would face the threat of proportionately stellar amounts. Or, assume that we want to prevent attempts to forge the currency. If the national legislature were to enact a law mandating a life sentence without parole for anyone convicted of forgery, and perhaps also that all of the person's property would be confiscated, then it is very likely that no one would risk committing forgery. Or consider "carjacking," the stealing of a car when it is in use by the forceful eviction of the driver. If carjacking were treated as equivalent to, say, second-degree murder, we could then predict (at least in certain societies) that thieves would limit themselves to more traditional ways of stealing cars.

We cannot go all out for a world that functions in accordance with the Ideal of Perfect Deterrence in all spheres in which punishment would be relevant and with every constituency. We would have to acknowledge pragmatic limits: for example, drug users under the total burden of their addiction may not be deterred from petty theft whenever it can support their habit, whatever the sanctions. There would also be ethical limits, such as not threatening to harm the criminal's family. And there are various other reasons to doubt whether perfect deterrence can be met often, primarily because people are irrational and self-deceptive in various ways. But we shall focus here on those instances where the proposal might apply and, in any case, the interest in the paradox remains even if it is mostly theoretical.

A crucial ingredient in applying the deterrence point is that people must have full assurance that, so long as they do not commit crimes, they will not be punished. As H. L. A. Hart put it, "For the system which makes liability to the law's sanctions dependent upon a voluntary act not only maximizes the power of the individual to determine by his choice his future fate; it also maximizes his power to identify in advance the space which will be left open to him free from the law's interference" (1970: 181–2). Achieving this goal would depend on mechanisms such as requiring the state to prove conclusively in court that that specific person has committed the crime. The law would also allow certain excuses from punishment to be available to the perpetrator, and it would include other safeguards. We need to assume, for the sake of our thought experiment, the complete and dependable existence of all such conditions. Similarly, we are assuming that the threat of punishment is used only in order to prevent genuine crimes and not, say, as a mechanism in the service of political oppression or religious orthodoxy.

Now we can see the Paradox of Non-Punishment:

1 At the deterrence point, no crime of type X is committed, and therefore no punishment for Xing occurs (since no one commits X). If there is no crime, and no punishment, things are ideal.

2 Nevertheless, we do not want a perfect deterrence point on such terms. We would view with horror a mature system of justice that threatens radically severe and disproportional punishment.

Let us now explore some possible arguments opposing a system of punishment based on perfect deterrence. First, someone might argue that perfect deterrence is unjust. There is something in this charge for, after all, a world that exhibits the Ideal of Perfect Deterrence threatens a level of punishment that goes beyond desert. However, this move at once confronts the difficulty that, since no one is being punished, there is, in fact, no injustice. A law can be unjust even if it is never applied. But someone can hardly be a victim of unjust punishment when no punishment occurs! Under perfect deterrence, Cicero would have nothing to worry about. Unlike traditional consequentialist suggestions, where punishment achieves good social results through actual injustice ("punishment" of the innocent, or the unjustly severe punishment of the guilty), in the case of perfect deterrence there can be no such injustice, since no one is to be punished in order to deter others from crime. Likewise, no one is being used (in the Kantian phrase) "only as a means" for the good of others, or sacrificed for their sakes. The admittedly serious problem of injustice that would occur were the punishment meted out is prevented from the start through the threat of that very punishment.

Second, what if someone *were to* commit a crime? Then indeed he or she will confront an unhappy and unjust prospect. Here I can reply in two ways. The first reply remains on the theoretical level. Even when dealing with a case in which it is completely certain that deterrence will work, most people would still object to the actual threat of overpunishment that is proposed. So the fear that someone will be caught in the net cannot be doing all of the intuitive work in making us reject the proposal to pursue the Ideal of Perfect Deterrence. This result suffices for my purposes. We can learn about morality, as we do about physics or economics, by playing with models that imitate ideal conditions. Second, we can surely think of cases in which, empirically, deterrence will be foolproof. In these cases, the deterrence is so strong that one would have to be literally crazy to succumb to committing the crime. Such obvious derangement might for that very reason be dealt with in a different manner. Moreover, even if a convicted person (who *is* guilty, after all) were to be severely punished by an adequately constructed system of justice which generally exhibits the Ideal of Perfect Deterrence, this overpunishment would be rare. Additionally, its importance would be negligible when compared to the evils of the current arrangements, where both crime and the suffering of punished criminals abound, in part as a consequence of the fact that societies consistently fail to provide incentives that are sufficient to deter crime. And, surely, in the proposed system the risks of punishing the innocent would decline considerably as compared to the current one.

A third argument might be based on fear. If people feared that they would suffer punishment at the draconian level of the deterrence point were they to commit the crime, this would haunt their lives. This possibility, however, is very much exaggerated. Admittedly, the institutional setting for overpunishment, and the intention to carry out the threats, would be there were someone to commit the given crime. This is required in order

Saul Smilansky

for the threat to be taken seriously. However, if people knew that the justice system provides an environment in which the innocent will not be harmed, then they would not commit crimes, remain innocent, and feel secure. A further response that might be made to the argument based on fear is that in adequate systems of justice it's even now possible that people will be punished for crimes they did not commit, and even (in some societies) possible that a person will be executed for a crime he didn't commit, yet few live in fear of that happening to him or her.

Fourth, it might be thought that the agency of individuals is affected when matters function in accordance with the Ideal of Perfect Deterrence, so that their decision-making processes are illicitly overwhelmed. Under the conditions that apply with the Ideal of Perfect Deterrence, after all, a large number of crimes that would have been committed in our current system are blocked, yet only the threat of extreme punishment prevents those crimes from occurring. But this argument is doubly faulty. Its logic would apply also to the fact that people are now deterred from crime because of their fear of the prevailing levels of punishment. It is wrong to commit crimes: if someone desists from crime because of the threat of punishment, that seems to be a good result. I do not see how one could plausibly argue that society owes the potential criminal an option to be punished less severely (namely, according to currently prevailing arrangements) just so that this person may more easily decide to commit a crime.

The threat of overpunishment with which we are concerned thus significantly differs from that of pre-punishment. Christopher New (1992) proposed that we may punish a person before he commits a crime when we know beyond a reasonable doubt that the person is going to commit it, and when we also know that we will be unable to punish him after he commits it. I replied (Smilansky 1994d) that such pre-punishment runs counter to the idea of respect for persons, according to which we must let the (still innocent) person decide, even at the last moment, to refrain from committing the crime, thus allowing her to maintain

The Paradox of Non-Punishment

her moral goodness and not be punished. But the idea of respect for persons does not seem capable of performing a similar role here since, again, no one is owed the threat of lesser punishment just so that he may more easily take up crime.

Moreover, it is misleading to describe a situation of perfect deterrence as one in which agency is overwhelmed. The Ideal of Perfect Deterrence does not operate through some sinister mechanism of brainwashing or through intervening chemically in the brain. The government in such a world does not invade anyone's privacy, nor does it bypass or modify anyone's agency or autonomy. Everything remains as matters are now: the agent is untouched. By upping the ante for a given crime, say, from $50 to $5,000, or from two years on probation to 12 years in prison, we have merely provided the potential criminal with a further rational reason to choose freely not to commit the crime.

Using the deterrence point is actually doing a favor to certain kinds of potential criminals: those who are deterred by the increased threats but would have committed the crime under the old rules. We are saving them from the crime and, if they are caught, the punishment.

The idea of a system of justice that in its very essence threatens people with radically severe and disproportionate punishment is distasteful. Yet, within the spheres where perfect deterrence can be applied, both crime and punishment are prevented. That is what makes perfect deterence attractive. The criminal justice system aims to prevent crime. If this can be done, and its achievement does not even require that anyone pay the price of being punished, then what is there to complain about? Compare this to a situation where the very thought of the prospect of taking medicine, if one were to become ill, would prevent all illness: wouldn't that be wonderful? Our current system, which involves high levels of both crime and punishment, is also distasteful, and the need for it is not attractive at all. We have yet to see a compelling principled reason for rejecting the Ideal of Perfect Deterrence (under the "Hartian" constraints mentioned earlier).

One possible reason, prominent in Catholic thinking, which has come up in discussions of nuclear deterrence, concerns intention.

Saul Smilansky

In order for such deterrence to be effective an intention to do the wrong (kill civilians en masse) must be formed, and the very formation of the intention can be said to be morally wrong. For good discussions see, e.g., McMahan (1985); Kavka (1987: ch. 2). The case of punishment that we are considering is very different: it is focused on punishing the guilty, typically would not involve the threat of death, is not intended to prevent social annihilation, is repetitive, is made by a system of justice, and so on. Such basic differences may help explain why nuclear deterrence is widely practiced and accepted, while threatening with gross and excessive punishment is shunned. Nevertheless, a similar reason based upon the wrongness of the intention to do wrong might be put forward here, in opposition to overpunishment. But this worry does not seem too weighty, except within certain theological assumptions: I doubt if a hypothetical intention can be so morally wrong, when it will not be actualized. And if it is actualized on some rare occasion, then the overpunishment itself (and not the intention) is what matters. I cannot enter into theological considerations here.

The proposal that we seek perfect deterrence through the justice system where we can achieve it, by using the threat of overpunishment, naturally arouses strong opposing intuitions. So long as we feel that we cannot overcome these intuitions, and continue to stand by our current practices, we confront the Paradox of Non-Punishment.

Arguably, we confront paradoxicality in any case. It seems paradoxical not to choose a way in which we can prevent both crime and punishment (we perfectly achieve the desired aim of the criminal justice system even without punishing anyone). But it also seems paradoxical to choose a process based upon the Ideal of Perfect Deterrence, since we are then saying that a system of justice ought to threaten people with radically severe and disproportionate punishment, which is far beyond what they deserve, in a way that would be manifestly unjust if the threat were to be carried out.

Civilized Western societies seem to have designed systems of justice that function by punishing criminals in a restrained fashion as the society's primary means of reducing crime. But the prospect of perfectly deterring crime in certain spheres by using the threat of radically severe punishment confronts us with a paradox. It seems unreasonable not to construct a system of justice that can prevent crime without actually punishing anyone (it makes both crime and punishment disappear together). But it also seems morally unacceptable to construct a system of justice that functions primarily by threatening its citizens with unjust punishment, while the justification for the system is dependent on the thought (even if it is true) that its threats will never need to be carried out.

Saul Smilansky

6 On Not Being Sorry about the Morally Bad

The sentiments of others can never affect us, but by becoming, in some measure, our own.
David Hume, *A Treatise of Human Nature*

Bad things often happen, and morally good people ought to regret that they happen. People are sometimes morally permitted not to do anything about such bad things, not to have to struggle to prevent them from occurring; otherwise the demands of morality would be excessive. But what could be more obvious than that a morally good person ought to be sorry about the occurrence of bad things? Even more so, it would seem, if the bad things occur in one's vicinity, or one is involved with them. I shall argue that sometimes it is morally permissible not to be sorry when bad things happen. It is even permissible to be happy about it. But how *can* morality say this?

Consider a case that is unambiguously bad. Before you were born your parents gave birth to a seemingly normal daughter, except that she was born with a severe defect in her heart, which led to her death after only a few weeks. Let us bracket the effect on your parents. You were born afterwards. In time, you learned that, had your sister survived, your even having been conceived would have been precluded. Are you sorry that she died? I am, in fact, that child, born because my sister died shortly after she was born and, all in all, I am not sorry that she did. But put yourself in my shoes and consider your own reaction.

The death of the baby is, of course, a bad event. By contrast, if you were the "possible" younger brother or sister in such a situation your not having been born would not have been bad. The number of times that babies are not conceived is literally uncountable, and this fact, barring a very unusual story, is not plausibly thought of as sad, let alone bad. Yet I do not see that you should be sorry that things happened as they did. Gloating would be inappropriate, and you can and should be sorry for her in the sense of feeling sympathy and pity (as well as regret that your existence depended on her death, and counter-factual regret that things could not have turned out such that both of you could have been alive). But in the overall sense, you are permitted not to be sorry that things have happened as they have. To distinguish the two senses, we can call the first sense of sorry "sorry *for*," and the second "sorry *that*." You ought to be sorry *for* her, but you are permitted not to be sorry *that* things (including her death) have happened as they did, for then you would not be alive. You are even morally permitted to be happy to have been born, even though you know that, for your birth to have occurred, your sister had to have died.

Nothing in this implies that you would be permitted (in some strange science-fiction sort of way) to bring about her death. Yet it also seems that you may permissibly not be sorry that she died. This despite the fact that not only is her death bad in itself, it is bad *overall* that she died; again, this is a worse state of affairs than her continuing to live and your not having been conceived. In this way, morality is much more lenient than we usually suppose. It is one thing to emotionally "accept" bad parts of one's own life (even dramatically bad parts, as we saw in Fortunate Misfortune), but quite another to "accept" (or even welcome) the bad in other people's lives. Yet such emotional "acceptance" of others' calamities is sometimes acceptable to morality, even when those calamities are bad overall.

I note in passing that there are two common but divergent intuitions about the term "morally bad." Under the narrower understanding, for an occurrence to be morally bad it needs to involve a person having done something morally wrong. Under the broader understanding, we could also speak of bad occurrences as "morally bad," although no one did anything morally wrong, because events (such as natural catastrophes) that morality deplores occur. I favor the broader interpretation, but nothing substantial hangs on this.

It may be useful if people believe that they always ought to be sorry about the occurrence of bad things, and that they certainly must not be happy about them. Strong human tendencies towards hatred, malevolence, envy, and cold indifference certainly need to be countervailed. But this is a different matter. The case of the baby shows that in certain cases one may permissibly not be sorry about the occurrence of bad things, *even when the only reason one could be not-sorry is that one gains from this.*

Surely there would be limits. Many people were born because their parents met while fleeing Nazi persecution. While their births would almost certainly not have occurred except for the Holocaust, one cannot morally be glad that the Holocaust occurred. The magnitude of suffering, loss, and evil are too great. The numbers count. It is in fact plausible to think that because of the disruptive effects of large events the scope of the argument here is more widespread, and millions of people would not have been born but for the Holocaust, and similarly for other catastrophes in history (see the "nonidentity problem"; Parfit 1984: ch. 16). Reflection on events on the historical scale means that we could not be happy that history occurred as it did, even if without some great calamity we and our loved ones would not have been born.

We should not think that our conclusion about the case of the baby follows from some curiosity or from an odd point of view on this case. Assume that a crazed gunman happens to open fire in your direction on the street. By chance two pedestrians step into the line of fire, thus dying, but your life is thereby saved (that both were hit was necessary for the bullets not to have reached you). Morally, the death of two people is worse than the death of one, even though that one would have been you. You ought to be sorry *for* those two people, but need you be sorry, overall, *that* things happened as they did? I do not think so. In fact, quite often we are not sorry implicitly when such things occur, if a bit less dramatically. If I am successful in love, or win that breakthrough job, this often follows from the fact that my competitor has had something bad happen to him or her (say, he or she had a mental breakdown, or was just not born too bright or attractive). Outside of the context of competition, I may wish him or her well, but within this specific context I am not sorry, all things considered, to have the upper hand. Typically we do not (or would not, if we could) do anything to change things, we do not think that we must change them, and we are not sorry to be as well off as we are, when bad things occur to other people. To our credit, we do not often think about these things in this way ("I am so pleased that he failed, because I thereby received that chance"); and would often feel some ambivalence (cf. Greenspan 1980). But if someone were to reflect on his or her responses in such competitive situations and declare that he or she is, overall, sorry (in the "sorry that" sense) to have won, we would suspect that person was being hypocritical.

Certain types of egalitarians and (for different reasons) utilitarians would be more strongly committed here. Because of the nature of their positions, they very often would – or, at least, should – be sorry that bad things happened to others rather than to themselves. But that statement might only be a *reductio* of those positions.

Consider now a different sort of case, in which very bad things happen to morally bad people. Such cases are also relevant for us, since the bad that befalls these persons may be very disproportional to what they deserve. A group of racist neo-Nazis, consumed with hatred for Jews and blacks, are glad about the suffering or death of any Jewish or black person, yet do nothing seriously bad to any Jewish or black person. On a certain day, members of this group (and no others) are traveling on a bus that swerves on the road and falls off a cliff. Death is

Saul Smilansky

a punishment that seems to go beyond even what virulent but passive racists deserve. Hence their death is a bad thing. It is bad, overall, that they died. Ought Jews and blacks to be sorry that they died? Or, indeed, ought they to be sorry for them? That seems excessive. Similarly, think about a case in which a rapist escapes justice, but then falls into the hands of thugs, who torture him. We can assume that torture is morally forbidden, certainly in such a case. But ought the women whom the rapist raped be sorry for him? Owing to special facts about the person involved (an "agent-relative" component), sometimes a person is permitted not to be sorry when morally bad things occur to others. In the cases of the neo-Nazis and of the rapist, not being sorry in both senses (sorry *for* and sorry *that*) seems permissible.

We do seem to be able to make distinctions here and to understand why it is sometimes permissible not to be sorry, or even to be happy, at the occurrence of bad things, and sometimes it is not. When the 9/11 terrorist attacks on the Twin Towers in New York occurred, it was widely remarked that many people around the world were happy about the events. There is room to consider who, if anyone, may (morally) be happy about these events, but clearly such happiness is very problematic. It is not like that of the victims of rape who are happy about the fate befalling their tormentor: the civilian victims of 9/11 were not responsible for harming the terrorists, or those who were happy about the events. Likewise, being happy at the gratuitous death of babies would in most cases count as a monstrous response, as it is not when the death of a baby happened to be a condition of your having been born. Our focus will be on the clear cases where not being sorry, or even being happy, about the morally bad is seemingly approved by morality – paradoxically.

Who may be happy about bad things in the way that we have considered? I favor a narrow interpretation. We may be tempted to enlarge the "permission" not to be sorry about the morally bad: shouldn't everyone, and not only Jews and blacks, be upset about the neo-Nazis? Ought not all people, and not only their victims, to condemn the rapists? Indeed we all should, but the

On Not Being Sorry about the Morally Bad

question at stake here is not that of the dislike and condemnation of bad people. Rather, we are concerned with the much more problematic thought that one may not regret, and may even be joyful, when morally bad things happen to these bad people. For instance, we are thinking about joy when they are wronged and made to suffer much beyond what they deserve. Here I think that tolerating such attitudes must be limited to those who are in some sense the direct victims or targets of the bad people, although there is perhaps some moral leeway here (extending the "permission" to family members?), and certainly questions as to how this idea should be interpreted. Perhaps in some limited way we may all not be sorry *for* such people, but most of us ought to be sorry *that* they were harmed so disproportionably. After all, something morally bad has happened. Some other factor might be doing part of the intuitive work: perhaps what makes us respond in this way is the belief that the bad guys will either be harmed more than they deserve or go completely free, and we wish to prevent, or are angry about, the latter prospect. Otherwise it is difficult to see why we would think that people may be happy when morally bad things happen to people who are unrelated to them. Such broad and easy negative emotions also surely create a risk of a "spill-over" into action. But note that even if one is inclined to disagree with this and enlarge the "permission" here, this would not harm the paradox but, on the contrary, would only make it more poignant. For, if no one is permitted to kill a bad person, but everyone (and not only some special and limited category of persons) is permitted to be happy when he is murdered, then matters are even more paradoxical than I have claimed.

Four objections to my claim, that morality can accept lack of regret or even happiness about the morally bad, can be anticipated. First, one could doubt whether deciding to be sorry or not sorry is at all within our power, thus putting it beyond the reach of moral consideration. This, however, is implausible. At issue here is not some deeply emotional response, but merely the basic sentiment that (if asked about it) one regrets that something is the case. We can understand that we have moral reason to be sorry about certain occurrences, and we *do* have some ability to affect attitudes of this sort. Moreover, this criticism clearly goes too far: surely we want to say that someone who is not bothered by the gratuitous murder of children, or becomes happy when he learns that a ship filled with old Buddhist or Muslim people sank, and they all drowned, is (if sane) morally at fault. Morality does aim to get people to restrain their behavior even when they have morally unacceptable emotions. But this should not obscure from us the point that being happy about certain things would be morally inappropriate (or worse).

Second, the perspectival and biased nature of our emotions can be put forward as making my claim to be "no big deal." After all, we are typically permitted to care more about those close to us and for our emotions not to be closely tracking impersonal value. It is natural to be saddened by the death even of one's pet, out of all proportion to the objective moral weight of the loss, and morality permits it. This, however, is not quite the same thing. At issue in this chapter is the idea that people may be not at all sorry (or may even be happy) at the occurrence of something morally bad or wrong, such as undeserved death or torture. But while people's reactions will be in clear *opposition* to morality on issues of great importance, even when fundamental moral constraints have been breached, morality permits this. And that, if true, is surely surprising.

Third, it might be thought that the cases I raised present nothing but the familiar idea of agent-centered priority and agent-centered permissions. For example, if a boat we are traveling on capsizes, we are allowed to save our loved ones even if we could instead save a larger number of strangers (thereby bringing about an objectively better state of affairs). However, this objection misidentifies the nature of the examples: we are not permitted to kill the baby (who dies shortly after birth), or the neo-Nazis (whose bus falls off a cliff). In the random shooting we are not permitted to push two bystanders into the line of fire in order to try to shield ourselves. Morality does not allow us to cause these deaths (as it does allow us not to prevent the deaths of the strangers that we do not save because we have instead saved our loved ones). Yet I have argued that it would not be morally wrong for relevant parties not to be sorry, in a central sense, about the deaths of the baby, the neo-Nazis, or the unlucky pedestrians. This apparent fact, that morality approves one's being happy over something bad that it would not allow one to do, lies at the heart of the perplexity.

Finally, it might be claimed that moral seriousness precludes my conclusion. If we are committed to morality then we must be sorry in the sort of cases that I presented; our attitudes ought to track our moral judgments. It is mere hypocrisy to avow morality but not to expect of oneself the appropriate reaction towards the occurrence of the bad. But this absolutist view seems too strong. I think that my examples make a convincing case for setting limits to the moral expectation for sorrow, even from those who are moral. When one cannot reasonably be expected to feel sorrow (at least sorrow overall, sorrow *that*), perhaps the call for sorrow is itself a mere call for hypocrisy.

Bad things happen even to good, innocent people. States of affairs that are bad overall often prevail. And people are morally wronged by others. But it may be all right not to be sorry, and we may even be allowed to be happy. Morality does not seem to demand that good people always be sorry when morally bad things happen. Quite how this can be so, when we ought to be sorry and when we may not, and when lack of regret may even turn to happiness about the morally bad, are difficult and important questions, which we have begun to explore, but which await further inquiry. Our emotions matter greatly in forming our moral behavior and in allowing us to live with morality's demands. The absence of sorrow and the happiness about the misfortune of others has clearly been conducive to the evils of history, such as slavery, economic oppression, anti-Semitism, and violent religious and nationalistic conquest. The struggle against such happiness at others' misfortune is central for morality. And yet in some cases, we have discovered, such lack of sorrow, and even happiness, is approved by morality.

Saul Smilansky

7 Choice-Egalitarianism and the Paradox of the Baseline

It is unjust if people are disadvantaged by inequalities in their circumstances, but it is equally unjust for me to demand that someone else pay for the costs of my choices.
Will Kymlicka, *Contemporary Political Philosophy*

Many people find current levels of inequality to be unjust, and support a "pro-equality" (or "egalitarian") stance. We shall explore the merits of an egalitarian view that has dominated the contemporary philosophical debate, called "luck-egalitarianism" or, as I prefer to call it, "choice-egalitarianism." Choice-egalitarianism is an egalitarian position that gives free choice a pivotal role. Unlike previous egalitarian positions, choice-egalitarianism seemed to take proper account of the role of choice and responsibility in moral justification. For example, if a person requires more social resources because he freely makes himself dependent upon an unequal share of such resources, others are not required to finance his choice. If he develops in himself a taste for expensive goods, or repeatedly squanders his resources in risky business gambles, others need not pick up the tab for his irresponsibility. Choice-egalitarianism also seemed more or less compatible with a market economy and a society that enables individual self-development through open and diverse choices. The prospect of such value synergy between equality, choice, responsibility, and efficiency was attractive to me, until I began to see what consistency in holding onto choice-egalitarianism would imply here.

The basic idea of choice-egalitarianism is this. We can morally evaluate equality and inequality in many respects: income, the existence of certain goods, well-being, and so on. Call these *factors*. Whatever the relevant factor that we are evaluating may be, the baseline for egalitarianism is equality: our evaluation starts, normatively, by assuming that everyone should receive the baseline, unless the person's not receiving it can be justified. In *choice*-egalitarianism the only acceptable justification for someone's not receiving the baseline rests on his or her free choice. For example, when the factor being equalized is access to some form of higher education without having to pay, a person may freely choose not to attend college. Someone who does not go to college because he does not like studying (but prefers surfing) admittedly ends up without a college education. The choice-egalitarian does not find this consequence objectionable, for it follows from that person's free choice.

A helpful version of choice-egalitarianism is G. A. Cohen's idea that egalitarians ought to strive for "equality of access to advantage" (Cohen 1989). Since virtually the only way in which inequality can be justified is through free choice (p. 931), inequality that does not result from "genuine choice" is a moral problem: the problem of the injustice of the arbitrary ways in which people become disadvantaged. He writes: "a large part of the fundamental egalitarian aim is to extinguish the influence of brute luck on distribution . . . Brute luck is an enemy of just equality, and, since effects of genuine choices contrast with brute luck, genuine choice excuses otherwise unacceptable inequalities" (p. 931). The difficulty at the core of choice-egalitarianism arises in connection with Cohen's position as well as other choice-egalitarian positions (see, e.g., Arneson 1989, but see also Arneson 2000; Rakowski 1991; Temkin 2003).

Among the potential difficulties with choice-egalitarianism, the most obvious lies in the notion of free choice. The complexities of the free will problem thereby become crucial for choice-egalitarians (see Smilansky 1997a; 2000: ch. 5, sec. 6.3).

Saul Smilansky

A second set of difficulties concerns the factors. If the factor is disability insurance, then equalizing it is perhaps not very problematic, but if we say that every person ought to be as happy as any other, then more serious difficulties arise (see, e.g., Smilansky 1995b). For instance, happiness often depends on one's love life, but attempting to equalize everyone's love life would be inherently problematic. I shall assume here that choice-egalitarianism can make sufficient sense of its basic notions of free choice as well as of the factors that need to be considered. The different challenge to choice-egalitarianism that I consider concerns the implications of the way in which the idea of a baseline functions in the theory.

Nothing is inherently problematic about the idea of a baseline, a concept that is used in considering many topics other than egalitarianism. We can think of a baseline merely as a helpful normative tool. Baselines come in many forms. The baseline can be in the middle, and a person can be either below it or above it, being inadequate in both cases but for opposite reasons: Aristotle's idea that virtues lie in a mean between two extremes is one such example. Sometimes the baseline is low, and one can move only upward from it. Volunteer work is optional rather than one's moral duty, so the baseline for volunteering is not-volunteering: if one volunteers to serve good causes, one is above the baseline, whereas if one does not volunteer, one is not below the baseline. Sometimes the baseline is at the top. In this form, justification is required for not being at the top: "above" is impossible and "below" requires justification. When we say that every person should be considered innocent until proven guilty, we are using innocence as our baseline in this way. Likewise for most human rights: certain basic liberties constitute a baseline that requires strong justification if we rescind them.

In egalitarianism, the normative baseline is equality, and divergence from this baseline requires justification. Justice, then, is comparative among persons, for we compare people in the relevant respects, and inequality between them needs to be justified. To this, choice-egalitarianism adds that the only acceptable justification for any inequality, for example, for a person's having less than others, is that the person has freely chosen it. (On the way in which the notion of the baseline operates in these contexts, see Smilansky 1996a, 1996b.)

More precisely, *if A is worse off than B in terms of factor F, choice-egalitarianism requires that A had an opportunity to be as well off as B in factor F, and A is not as well off solely because of A's free choices.*

Consider income. What is the normative baseline for evaluating inequalities, according to choice-egalitarianism? A first approximation is: the highest income that anyone possesses. Let us call this Highest Income. Whatever that may be, choice-egalitarianism holds that everyone ought to have an identical income, unless a given person's free choice led her to attain less. Arguably the baseline is located even higher. Perhaps, for choice-egalitarianism, the baseline is the earning level of the persons most able to earn high incomes *if* those persons were to decide to work as hard as they could at the position at which they could have the highest income. Let us call this Highest Potential Income.

Here is the reason for our considering Highest Potential Income and not only Highest Income. Assume that Maxi can earn a fortune pursuing her chosen career in the open market, but decides to work only half-time. She is then earning only half of her potential. Mini, on the other hand, cannot earn very much, and certainly not as much as Maxi, for reasons beyond her control. According to choice-egalitarianism, society must clearly top up Mini's earnings so that she earns as much as Maxi earns. Otherwise Mini will be earning much less and this will not be justified by her free choices. But even if Mini were capable of earning as much as Maxi, she might not wish to work only half-time; she might want to actualize her earnings potential. Let us assume that this is what she would do. If we use only Highest Income as our baseline, we neglect this inequality between the earning potential of Mini and of Maxi, which similarly is not in any way a result of Mini's free choices. Hence Highest Potential Income seems to be the baseline that choice-

Saul Smilansky

egalitarianism requires. However, even Highest Income suffices to let the paradox be revealed.

Consider now the group of people who are almost completely impotent in the world: however hard they try, however positive their motivation and constant their efforts, they will not be able to gain most types of the goods that we have called "factors." For instance, they are so disabled that no one within a market economy has the slightest self-interested incentive to hire their services. Under capitalism, therefore, these people cannot generate any sort of income. Call these people Non-Effectives (NEs).

At this stage paradox strikes. According to choice-egalitarianism, Non-Effectives ought to get the baseline of Highest Income, or even Highest Potential Income, since the basic moral implication of choice-egalitarianism is that *no one may have a higher income than Non-Effectives.* For if anyone does, this inequality cannot be justified by the free choices of those Non-Effectives who are worse off (by definition of what an NE is). Hence, for choice-egalitarianism, the social order in terms of income (or resources, or well-being, or whichever factors are to be equal under choice-egalitarianism) will find Non-Effectives at the top, for they are permanently and unconditionally "stuck" at the baseline. People who are not Non-Effectives (Not-NEs, i.e. Effectives) will have progressively less and less income, according to the extent to which they fall short of Highest Income (or Highest Potential Income) by freely choosing to work less, or by choosing not to develop their income-enhancing abilities further, or by their other free choices.

Choice-egalitarianism promised to be a workable position that can accommodate a free society and a market economy. Once we see how high its baseline must be, and the peculiar role that choice plays in determining where one will be in relation to the baseline, such hopes for a "workable egalitarianism" can be seen to be misplaced, as the following features of a just social order under choice-egalitarianism make clear:

1   In terms of possessing some relevant factor (e.g., the highest income and the greatest resources), the persons at the top

will be Non-Effectives. No one will have a higher income or more resources than any Non-Effective. Their receiving the baseline, high though it may be, would be *unconditional.*

2   The high income that Non-Effectives will receive is calculated by being indexed to whoever has Highest Income (or Highest Potential Income) when the economic game plays out. Let us call this person "Bill Gates." This person's income will fluctuate, but the Non-Effectives' income will track it.

3   There will be no adequate relation between what a person achieves and contributes to others, and what level he or she occupies in terms of incomes and resources: in fact, a whole category of persons who contribute nothing will always be at the top of the scale (together with Bill Gates).

4   Significant inequality will exist at every level below that which the Non-Effectives (and Bill Gates) occupy, because most Effectives (those with the potential to contribute and earn if they work hard) will fall back from the baseline, to various degrees, due to their free choices (see Fig. 7.1).

5   The Effectives will have to finance the income of the Non-Effectives (and, to a lesser extent, partial Non-Effectives, and so on). But it is highly unlikely that the Effectives will ever reach as high as the baseline, where the Non-Effectives will automatically reside.

Here, then, is the Paradox of the Baseline. For choice-egalitarianism, Non-Effectives must necessarily be at the baseline of Highest Income (or even Highest Potential Income), while Effectives are very likely to fall much below the baseline in spite of their lifelong efforts and contributions. Choice-egalitarianism indexes every Non-Effective to Bill Gates (or even to what his income would be were he to meet his maximal earnings potential), while hard-working and effective people are very unlikely to come even close. This means that choice-egalitarianism cannot give Non-Effectives what it must, and at the same time do comparative justice to hard-working Effectives. That is something that ought to trouble egalitarians, irrespective of the question of

Saul Smilansky

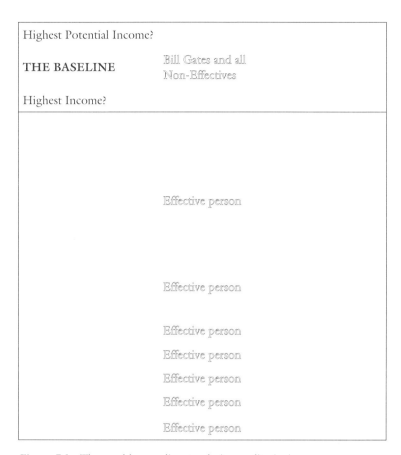

Figure 7.1 The world according to choice-egalitarianism.

how it affects the issue of whether their position may still be attractive to others. The obligation to position the Non-Effectives as high as Bill Gates cannot be reconciled with the moral need to maintain a reasonable relation between the positions of Non-Effectives and Effectives. These two requirements are contradictory. Moreover, choice-egalitarianism "penalizes" choosing ability, for it leads to the conclusion that those who are in a position to make choices that could enhance their incomes and their abilities to contribute to the well-being of others are very likely to fall well below the level that is to be unconditionally occupied by those who cannot make such choices.

This vision is both absurd and morally repugnant. The prospect that it (or any view that approaches it) might be applied to a free and modern society becomes impossible to entertain.

Matters become even more striking if one extends the factors that are thought to be pertinent beyond income or resources, narrowly understood. If, for instance, happiness or honor are the factors to be equalized, then no one (according to choice-egalitarianism) may be allowed to be happier than the greatest depressive, nor may anyone be honored more than the least respected person, whatever her achievements or contributions, unless the depressives or non-respected persons are such because of their free choices (see Smilansky 1995b). Kasper Lippert-Rasmussen (2004) attempts to defuse the paradox by focusing upon well-being rather than income or resources. For, in terms of the capacity for well-being, no one is strictly "non-effective." But as I argue in reply (Smilansky 2004), taking this direction would, overall, make matters worse for the egalitarian. The need for compensation would then not stop with income (even with Bill Gates's income); it would often be as good as infinite. It is best to think about these matters in terms of standard factors such as income and resources.

Two replies may seem to be available to the paradox. First, perhaps choice-egalitarianism need not use a "top" baseline such as I used in reaching the paradox. Why not, for instance, use a "middle" baseline? This might amount to a certain "decent" level of income or resources at which all citizens would reside. By their free choice (say, by deciding not to work) they would forfeit it, or be able to reach above it (say, by working extra hours). A social order with such a "middle" baseline would have many attractions for those with egalitarian sensibilities, among them that the income and resources of Effectives would depend on their choices, while the income and resources of Non-Effectives (who could not "play the game" and hence could not fall below the baseline) would be at the fairly high baseline despite their condition. There could surely be worse arrangements than this. Even so, this "middle" baseline proposal is inadequate from the choice-egalitarian perspective. If we take choice-egalitarianism seriously, then *any* person's being less well off than any other in terms of the pertinent factor needs to be explicable only through that first person's free choice (otherwise morally arbitrary forces beyond his or her control and not free choice determine what he or she gets). But this manifestly will not be the case in a "middle" baseline world, as here some people will be significantly better off than the Non-Effectives, while the Non-Effectives will not have had the choice to reach that much higher level. Hence only a "top" baseline does justice to the deep intuitions of choice-egalitarianism.[1]

Second, the choice-egalitarian can perhaps admit the paradox but attempt to defuse it by claiming that choice-egalitarianism is not proposed as a complete account of how a society should arrange its social and economic affairs. This is a sensible move, and choice-egalitarians have indeed limited the range of their proposal in this way. However, this will not do as a way of confronting the Paradox of the Baseline. The paradox does not threaten some marginal feature of the choice-egalitarian structure, or some feature that emerges only in the extremes of fully implementing it within social policy. On the contrary, the Paradox of the Baseline follows from the basic ethical structure of choice-egalitarianism, and it frames any social order that is based on it. The threat it poses is fundamental.

NOTE

1   Tal Manor (2005) embraces my *reductio* argument against choice-egalitarianism. He argues, however, that when the gap between the common man or woman and the baseline becomes large enough, almost everyone becomes a relative or partial Non-Effective. Indexing almost everyone to Bill Gates means radically lowering Gates's income, thereby yielding a strongly egalitarian outcome. In Smilansky (2005d) I argue that even today, let alone in an ideal choice-egalitarian society, most people in Western

societies are not Non-Effectives and need not be indexed to Bill Gates, for they have considerable choosing powers that they do not exercise. The absurdity of indexing the Non-Effectives to Gates thus remains, and those atypical instances where the indexing of not-Non-Effectives is required, increase the absurdity rather than decrease it.

Saul Smilansky

8 Morality and Moral Worth

And for morality life is a war, and the service of the highest is
a sort of cosmic patriotism.
  William James, "Circumscription of the Topic"

If the social environment were arranged so that most people
could be morally good with relative ease, would this be a good
thing? This is no idle question: some Western democratic societies today seem to be approaching a situation where morality is
not taxing. And it is not entirely obvious that we should say yes.
As in Fortunate Misfortune, the bad isn't always simply bad.
This question also has substantial theoretical interest because
exploring it can help us understand the paradoxical relationship
between morality and moral worth.

  I am construing "morality" in the narrow sense as a system
of constraints and obligations regarding one's behavior towards
others; I shall not consider here the idea of duties towards oneself.
Much recent philosophical discussion on ethical and political matters attempts to limit the demands that morality, in this sense,
ought to make on individuals. I ask a very different question,
about the attitude we should take to a state of affairs in which
there is no *need* for more than limited ethical demands.

Two Views of Morality

A most curious thing about common views of morality is their deep ambivalence: many people cherish morality as a basis for laudable moral behavior, while many other people deprecate it.

Laudatory views hold moral behavior to be the highest achievement of civilization, the hallmark of humanity's superiority over other species, the measure of one's personal worth as compared to others, and the like. When people act morally, and in particular when they follow the moral code for its own sake, sacrificing self-interest, they are said to be most deserving of admiration. As in so much else that concerns morality, this idea finds its strongest expression in Kant (1986: 60), but the attitude is not limited to him or even to Kantian thought. Utilitarians, too, hold the widely shared view that true moral action bestows great value on people, particularly when they act morally in demanding situations (e.g., Kagan 1989: ch. 10).

It is important to note that while the elucidation of such value achievable by moral behavior involves taking account of subjective components (such as how the agent perceived her situation), we have to set some objective standards for what we will consider as having moral value. If any trivial moral conformity would grant one high moral value, then the issue I raise would make no sense. When we speak about high moral value as an achievement, we are, then, referring to matters such as steeling oneself in order to do the morally good thing, even when there are very good self-interested reasons not to follow morality.

There are disagreements as to which of several versions of the laudatory point of view bestows the highest moral value. Some would take the detached objectivity of an impersonal "ideal observer" as the standard. Others esteem deep emotional involvement. Some see detachment from one's own concerns as the mark of the truly moral, others the enlargement of the self that encompasses the concerns of others. Some focus on the rationality of truly moral deliberation while others see morality as a matter for appropriate sentiments. Common to all these positions, however, is the view that, when people act morally, they are at their most admirable, and even that certain forms of value come into being *only* when people act in the light of moral concerns under trying circumstances. Moral behavior as I speak of it refers only to moral action performed for reasons that are morally estimable.

This laudatory view of moral behavior has proved surprisingly flexible. We are well aware that a significant amount of moral behavior reflects egoistic calculation, simple conformity, or even psychological pathology. Nevertheless, much moral behavior resists cynical deflation. Many people have experienced encounters in which they did not take improper advantage of others' weaknesses, not because they were afraid but because it would have been wrong to do so. Some people have sacrificed or risked much, in order to stand up for moral principles, or for the sake of the interests of others. These people may rightfully view such instances as sources of pride and value. The more extreme the case, the clearer this becomes, both to the participants and to any observers. One cannot remain cynical in the face of the actions of those in German-occupied Europe who, in a pervasive atmosphere of apathy, fear, or even sympathy with the Nazis, risked their lives to save complete strangers, with no prospect of reward. Or think about those courageous Italian individuals, particularly in the south of the country, who have struggled against the widespread influence of the Mafia, at obvious risk to their lives.

Deprecatory views of morality, by contrast, perceive morality as a burden, at best an unfortunate social necessity that obstructs the pursuit of more interesting and important matters. How good it would be if morality did not require sacrifices, if one's projects were not constantly interrupted by external moral requirements, if social needs that today make exacting moral demands could be met with only limited recourse to such demands. Here as well we can find distinct views: some, for instance, would emphasize the rights people have for minimal interference from other people, along libertarian lines. Others would stress the value of varied experiments in living and of the importance of self-development (liberals in the sense of John Stuart Mill). Yet others (such as

Nietzsche and Bernard Williams) see a constraint morality as we understand it here as inherently repressive, demeaning, and (for Nietzsche) exploitative. But with all the differences, the crucial point is that morality is best when it imposes least.

Whether we hold the laudatory or the deprecatory view of morality has far-reaching implications. If we consider morality the crown of humanity, we will see many issues differently than if we see morality as essentially a nuisance. A major difference between these two views will emerge as we consider the idea of ordering society so that our lives rarely involve demanding moral behavior. At issue here is not the implausible notion that morality in the limited interpersonal sense can simply wither away (Steven Lukes (1985) rejects this possibility convincingly) but rather that morality might become such that most people, as they currently are, would not find its constraints taxing.

Two Possible Moral Worlds

Let us delineate two possible moral worlds. The first is:

The well-arranged minimal-morality world

Assume that social arrangements and socializing processes could be directed in such a way that the burden that morality places on our behavior is limited. Certain basic requirements of personal interaction, such as telling the truth, would remain, but an ordinary law-abiding person could be considered perfectly decent if he or she were concerned only to a minimal degree with morality. No special manipulative or otherwise morally troubling effort would be involved in creating and maintaining this world. We are simply considering ordinary, run-of-the mill attempts to make things better, for example, to improve living conditions that would otherwise cause misery and crime, and hence require moral intervention. Matters would be arranged so that, to the extent that moral demands depend on broad social circumstances, it would become fairly easy to be good.

Saul Smilansky

Would this be a gain or a loss? According to the deprecatory view of morality this would be all to the good. Morality, after all, limits liberty and the pursuit of happiness, and sometimes threatens life as well. If each of us could get by without imposing on other people too much, and without being imposed upon by them very much, what more could we ask? This view regards moral behavior as a mechanism for achieving certain purposes, such as furthering the preferences of all individuals. If such goals, external to morality, can be achieved at a limited price in terms of moral requirements, it would seem that only moral fetishism could find fault here. Worse still, to demand more than that of moral behavior may indicate not only confusion between aims and means but perhaps even a morbid tendency to seek guilt, subservience, and self-mortification through morality. There are sound pragmatic reasons for people to develop respect for morality and appreciation for moral achievements but these concerns should not distract us. Considered rationally, morality is a useful but obstructive instrument that imposes constraints, and it ought to be treated accordingly.

To those whose view of morality is more laudatory, the meaning of such developments, which seem completely compatible with the deprecatory view, would be more ambiguous. If people could really live their lives by sacrificing only very little for the sake of strictly moral concerns, a loss would be involved. For if, in acting morally, human beings achieve the heights of value, a life without moral concerns and sacrifices would become relatively shallow and petty, in some respects at least. Arranging things so as to require very little serious concern about morality could be seen as a threat to human beings' attaining true human nobility.

It has been argued that overemphasis on morality in the West has impaired the quality and development of many lives. Great benefits could therefore accrue by cutting loose from some of the strictures in common morality, in the direction, for example, of an ethics of virtue (e.g., Williams 1985: ch. 10). Admittedly, if one takes an extremely denigrating view perhaps one can see no merit in either morality or moral behavior. But if we dismiss such extreme views because they fail to consider the potentially great value at stake, which we noted earlier as being intuitively appealing, more moderate criticism of morality would leave our issue intact. Even if one holds that common morality is constraining or otherwise harmful, I maintain that *there is a specific value that only moral behavior provides.* Claims about common morality or its overall benefits do not need to be defended here. I rely only on the persuasive idea that value, even a sort of beauty, emerges from truly moral behavior. This sort of value is specifically related to a particular way of being that relies on the familiar institution of morality, and thus it cannot be attained by imbuing life with additional content of a different nature.

The second possible moral world is:

The ill-arranged unnecessarily morally demanding world

Assume that ordinary morality were to remain in place, but in addition that it were legitimate to create situations that demand extreme moral endeavor. One would need only to create more hardship, suffering, and injustice, all of which are easy to arrange. Such unnecessary misery and evil would then provide ample opportunities for moral behavior to rectify it.

A sane morality would find any effort to create such a world unacceptable, even monstrous. A man whose "life project" is the eradication of some form of evil should not add to this evil even if there is less and less evil around, even if his project is being threatened.

We see that we should affirm the intrinsic value of much moral behavior while criticizing, for instance, those ideological or religious positions that call for externally unjustified sacrifices, sacrifices for which no independent moral need exists in the real world. Positions such as those suffer from three faults:

The first is normative. Such positions impose upon people unnecessarily, abusing the good will of human beings and disrupting their lives without properly justifying the moral need for doing so. This criticism accords with a basic intuition behind the deprecatory view of morality. It asserts that oppressive moral demands in the absence of strict necessity must be precluded.

Saul Smilansky

The second fault is empirical. Such positions naturally engender an increase (or at least prevent a decrease) in the evils that call for moral sacrifices. Unlike a broadly instrumental view of morality, such positions have a stake in the continuing existence of such evils. Hence, their proponents will often fail to combat them in good faith.

The third point is conceptual. Such positions threaten the purity of achieving moral value because they do not focus solely on the object of moral activity, that is, to relieve human suffering and eliminate grievous wrongs. Instead they tarnish moral value with other concerns that are self-oriented (or otherwise motivated), not morality oriented. There need be no objection to the personal satisfaction one gains from carrying out moral dictates. Morality welcomes the prospect of people who are happy to do good. But the value of moral behavior requires that moral agents focus on tasks at once beyond the self and concerned with real moral needs. *These* are the tasks that require moral action, and from which one can gain moral value.

The Reality of the Issue

The well-arranged minimal-morality world might be seen as a mere thought-experiment that hardly need engage us, but this is not so. It is dangerous to generalize about long-term social developments, but one sees the major thrust of democratization and modernization as progressively limiting how demanding individual morality needs to be. Matters are certainly not irreversible: new and incurable epidemic diseases or the rise to power of fascist parties in certain Western countries cannot be ruled out. The threats of terrorism and war can alter the situation. But the trend is clear nonetheless. This is where many advanced societies are trying to get to, and it seems likely that some of them will approach such conditions. The establishment of democratically accountable government, the defense of human rights within the rule of law, the displacement of the multigenerational family by the welfare state, the advances in medicine and in crop development, the widespread abolition of conscript armies, and the general reduction of extreme poverty, persecution, and injustice – all these have decreased the role of oppressive moral demands in our lives as individuals, and have largely eliminated the need for moral heroism. Obviously the potential for doing evil remains – people still molest children, for example. But in societies such as Denmark or New Zealand, say, one can generally get by without an undue burden of morality, both with respect to the contingencies of personal survival and in the need to confront social evils.

The major significant exception to this trend concerns the plight of the Third World. On this issue, positions such as extreme utilitarianism are exceedingly demanding even for people in the West. However, this extreme stand follows from the sense of the West's virtually limitless obligations to the Third World, including the belief that individuals in the West who are not poor must take up the obligations of other non-poor people who ought to contribute but do not.

Both positions can be disputed. But even if there were strong obligations to eliminate the plight of the poor in the Third World, these duties could in fact be met without overburdening individuals in the West. A limited increase in taxes by Western nations would suffice, thereby eliminating the need for great sacrifices by any given individual. Once the Third World issue is set aside, the practical relevance of the topic I am raising can be recognized. (Singer (1972) is the classic presentation of the demanding view on duties towards the Third World; L. Jonathan Cohen (1981) discusses the connection between what one ought to do and the inaction of others. Many recent discussions have followed those two paths.)

Compare the very different choices facing dissidents in the former Soviet Union or in Argentina under the Generals with those faced by activists in the democratic West during peacetime. Dedicated moral behavior in the democratic West is surely displayed in concern for local poverty, for Third World hunger, or for the environment. But there is no comparison in terms of the presence, weight, and unavoidability of the moral challenge.

Saul Smilansky

Major ethical dilemmas, such as whether to protest stark evils by risking one's life and the livelihood of oneself and one's family, were by and large real only in illiberal societies. And the friendships that emerged from a shared faith and the confrontation with evil and danger have scarcely any parallel in the democratic West. Such opportunities for moral achievement that depend on challenges and dangers exist only on the margins of well-ordered societies. Typically this is so on the less well-ordered margins, for example, in the fight against organized crime. In terms of the daily actuality of challenges that bring forth significant moral value, living in a well-ordered society such as we are considering is "bad moral luck."

It is not only that under difficult conditions there is more scope for action above and beyond the ordinary line of duty. The whole moral field is thrown into flux, challenging facile distinctions between one's duty and what lies outside it. Deliberating whether to betray friends when not to do so might mean entrapment and torture by the secret police, for instance, becomes a "natural" part of life. Hence, the challenge to remain or become moral is acute. My point, however, does not depend on such extreme situations. It is simply that when fear and suffering are limited, as is increasingly the case in the democratic West, the ethical climate is likely to be milder. The moral environment makes fewer demands for high principles, commitment, and courage. One becomes adequately moral with ease. Life tends to become easy, at least for the moderately affluent, and morally shallow, thereby affecting more general aspects of the development and maturation of personality.

We could anticipate that a world in which the special virtues would be brought forth would probably also be a world in which the corresponding vices would emerge more often. Situations that enable me to be especially altruistic also enable me to be especially selfish, and those in which I could manifest courage are also those in which I could also behave as a coward. But since we are interested here only in the potential for positive moral worth, and in the possibility of losing it in circumstances that are "too morally easy," I shall not pause to consider this.

Morality and Moral Worth

Needs, Moral Requirements, and Moral Worth: The Basic Logic

Both the deprecatory view, which resents obtrusive moral demands, and the laudatory view, which celebrates moral worth, have intuitive appeal. One views the need for moral behavior as an unfortunate disturbance, the other as a vital opportunity, but if we learn from their partial but valid insights, we can also make a case for seeing both of these opposing views of morality as to some extent true. In the most plausible view about morality, they are paradoxically interwoven. Moral behavior is the realm where people can be most admirable, where human value can be uniquely enhanced, but we can still view social morality as essentially instrumental, thereby aiming to limit its domain.

The value of moral behavior depends on there being a need for morality, but this need cannot consist in providing such value. That would get things backwards. The need for moral behavior is external: it arises when we encounter actual human suffering and grievous wrongs (morality isn't only about these two, but they will be representative for us of what matters). These in turn urge us to eliminate them as far as possible: they urge us to eliminate the circumstances responsible for the suffering and wrongs. However, doing so would thereby reduce opportunities for achieving moral value. If there are needs that are truly best met by making moral demands, morality should make such demands. But the needs are the starting point. The inner logic of the institution of morality, according to the view of morality that I am proposing, is broadly instrumental; this implies, however, that *it is inevitably geared towards reducing to a minimum those situations that, by making people cope with a demanding morality, enable them to achieve value.*

Our discussion may recall traditional efforts at theodicy, which have urged that a beneficial God would have to allow for evil in order for people to be able to exercise virtues such as forbearance, compassion, and charity, as well as meaningful free will. But the point here is that the logic of morality seems to require

Saul Smilansky

that human beings aim to solve moral problems, hence minimizing the need for subsequent sacrifice.

This view in no way implies that morality is unimportant or disreputable, or that people who behave morally are not to be admired. Given the need for moral behavior, those who meet this need are rightfully esteemed. Actually, it is the very fact that certain people meet real, external moral needs that gives moral content to their action. But this view can coexist with the recognition that morality is inherently purposeful, and that attempts should be made to limit the need for moral action.

One might think that the need for moral education and development undermines my case, for does not morality demand that we pose challenges to young people in order to develop their moral capacities and inclinations? This is part of what William James (1982) had in mind when he tried to convince us to look for the "moral equivalent of war," which could preserve worthwhile virtues, usually brought out in warfare, without the unnecessary bloodshed. Morality allows us to nurture values in people: given the need for moral agents, we are allowed to attempt to "produce" them (primarily when they are young and within other limitations). But morality focuses on external needs that necessitate moral behavior. We must not confuse the possibility of encouraging people to be moral in given circumstances with the attempt to create ethical value for its own sake. Morality does not allow us to create gratuitous moral difficulties merely so that they can be overcome.

Consider briefly another example. The recent development of synthesized meat products may make the killing of animals for culinary purposes redundant. This would eliminate the moral value some vegetarians currently get by abstaining from eating meat. One could still refrain from eating meat, but no genuine moral requirement would be met through this (for meat would no longer be connected to the killing of animals), and so no moral value would be gained. But of course we would not want to ban these new procedures in order to preserve the potential for vegetarian virtue.

Recall the well-arranged minimal-morality world. If most people could easily become "secular saints" as the result of an

Morality and Moral Worth

improved arrangement of the moral environment, one could not legitimately resist such a change simply on the grounds that the environment would become too "easy," too insufficiently challenging morally.

We can agree with those who insist on limiting the social demands that morality can make on individuals to those necessitated by actual external needs. We can agree as well that efforts should be made to reduce the imposition such social demands make on us, by seeking arrangements that make the harsher demands of morality unnecessary. Neither of these conditions requires us to deny the great value of moral behavior. In fact, insofar as external moral needs exist and are met because they exist, the purity of achieving moral value will be enhanced. This position combines the strong points of the laudatory and the deprecatory views of morality.

But even if we find this persuasive, we must not lose sight of the strangeness of the relationship of and interdependence between external needs, moral demands, and moral worth. External needs necessitate morality, and the moral demands thus generated, if met, confer the value of being moral. Moral worth is contingent on conditions that morality is obliged to try to eliminate. The purpose of true morality is to eliminate certain conditions (suffering and grievous wrongs). Yet only if those conditions exist can they call forth the moral actions that uniquely confer moral value. Paradoxically, morality is an "enemy" of moral worth. Valuable moral behavior ends up resembling one of those mythological animals that eat their own tails, thus putting an end to the very condition for their own existence.

The need for a morality that places demands on us, which must in itself be seen as dispensable, makes possible the creation of great intrinsic value, the value of moral behavior. Great and perhaps unique value emerges from true moral behavior, but the need for morality should be limited as much as possible. And so, the need for morality must be seen from one perspective as the consequence of an unfortunate imperfection. This mountain of imperfection creates the opportunity to mine the gold of moral behavior. But moral behavior cannot be a self-justifying value,

Saul Smilansky

cannot exist for its own sake. This circumstance is an inherent source of its value. Admirable moral action is parasitic on independently existing moral needs which, on the social level, morality should try to eliminate. One is tempted to say that if the evils that call forth admirable moral action did not exist, one would have to invent them, because only moral behavior can bestow great value of the sort that concerns us. But proponents of morality could never accept this.

9 The Paradox of Moral Complaint

For the only time a criminal cannot complain that a wrong is done him is when he brings his misdeed back upon himself, and what is done to him in accordance with penal law is what he has perpetrated on others, if not in terms of its letter at least in terms of its spirit.

Immanuel Kant, *Metaphysics of Morals*

When may people complain, morally? I want to point out a perplexity about a certain class of moral complaints. The issues we shall engage are as old and familiar as the "eye for an eye," the *lex talionis*, but focusing upon the relatively neglected notion of complaint is helpful. It makes it more difficult to take a standard "absolute constraint" (deontological) line, which forbids certain actions towards people whatever they have done, and hence it creates a dilemma and a paradox.

It is useful to think about the topic of moral complaint within the context of a view that sees morality as universally prescriptive. Let us assume:

L   The general "legislative" nature of morality and moral action.

The moral principles one puts forth apply equally to everyone, in relevantly similar circumstances. And actions count: when one performs morally significant actions, one thereby legislates, in

Saul Smilansky

some sense, that according to one's principles it is permissible for relevantly similar others to perform similar actions under similar circumstances.

Hence, when proposing some moral principle, or when proposing to act in ways that morally affect others, we should ask ourselves how we would feel, or how we would judge the situation, if others were to treat us in that way in similar circumstances. According to *L*, we should take our actions very seriously, for they may serve as moral precedents, and rebound against us.

Consider the following examples:

1   People who enjoy malicious gossip and frequently pass the gossip along to others often complain that those who gossip about them invade their privacy and spread untrue stories.
2   Violent criminals and those who sympathize with them often complain about police brutality, the injustice of the courts, and the dehumanizing conditions in prisons.
3   Terrorists and their defenders often complain about having no recourse to judicial appeal and about the unfair conditions of their detention, as they also complain when innocent persons they care about are killed.

The problem begins when we think about moral complaint in such cases. Two very different conceptions of moral complaint seem to underlie these cases, and both seem applicable. Each has implications that are contrary to those of the other. And both seem intuitively compelling. Both also seem to be interpretations of *L*. But even if one has doubts about *L*, the intuitive appeal of the following conceptions is strong.

N   The non-contradiction condition for complaint.

Morally, a person cannot complain when others treat him or her in ways similar to those in which the complainer freely treats others.

The Paradox of Moral Complaint

U The unconditional nature of some moral standards.

Some moral standards apply unconditionally. These standards allow anyone to hold others to them, and to complain if those others do not act in accordance with those standards.

I want to examine *N* and *U* in more detail, to show how they can both be thought to follow from *L*, and to account for their inherently strong intuitive appeal.

N: The Non-Contradiction Condition for Complaint

L implies that a person cannot morally complain about being treated in a way that is similar to the way in which that person freely treats others. If, by regularly spreading tales about the private affairs of others, one implicitly affirms one's moral position on the permissibility of gossip, then surely there is a sense in which one cannot complain about being the target of gossip.

If, by inflicting pain on people, one implicitly declares one's moral position on violence and cruelty, then one cannot complain about being treated according to the very ways that one implicitly deems morally permissible. Terrorists, who intentionally target innocent victims, and hence affirm the permissibility of doing so, cannot complain when they themselves are summarily treated or when subterfuge or violence is aimed at them. Nor can they speak about the sanctity of the lives of innocent civilians, on pain of inconsistency.

How *can* one morally complain about the very thing that one persists in doing to other people in relevantly similar circumstances? Surely the gossip decrying gossip, the criminal roaring against lawlessness and violence, and the terrorist concerned for the lives of the innocent, stand on extremely dubious ground. Why should we find their protests convincing? What basis can they have for moral indignation when they freely and repeatedly contradict their words through their actions?

I bracket here genuine contrition and repentance and, differently, weakness of will. If one had done wrong in the past but has reformed and now views one's past actions with horror, then the possibility of complaint may be more readily available to a person. A weak-willed person may complain about things done to him although he also does similar things to others, if he genuinely wants and tries not to do them but finds himself unable to stop. Such cases might allow complaint by wrongdoers, but these exceptions need not concern us.

Moral complaint occurs when my moral expectation is unmet in a way which I believe to be unjustified, and which I therefore resent. General moral principles that I assume others share (or ought to share) are the basis for moral complaint. But this becomes very problematic when another person's action that harms us is in accordance with our own actualized principles. Recall *L*. How can I morally resent or complain about another's doing to me as I freely do to him (unless unusual circumstances exist)? How can I morally resent or complain about his applying against me the moral rule that I myself have set? According to this interpretation of *L*, "Do not do unto others as you would not want them to do unto you" may turn into "And if you so do unto others and they so do unto you, you cannot complain." You condemn yourself to live as you have legislated.

The point is not only that it is natural not to feel sympathy for the gossip, criminal, or terrorist, when they complain about the very same sort of actions that they freely and regularly inflict upon others. The claim that they have on others, to morally care about the way in which they were treated, loses its footing. Through their gross disrespect of others, they have thereby lost the basis for complaint at being treated with similar disrespect. They lack the moral good will, as well as the integrity and consistency between their actions and demands from others, required in order to deserve our concern about their moral expectations. They assume in their complaint a principle that they have made abundantly clear they do not believe in. The wrongdoers have legislated in a way that precludes their own moral complaint, for there is no grounding for their complaint within that legislation.

The Paradox of Moral Complaint

U: The Unconditional Nature of Some Moral Standards

We feel that there are moral standards that apply "no matter what," and these allow even the most irresponsible gossip or the most sordid criminal or terrorist to hold us to them, and to complain if we do not apply them. The fact that those who are morally bad do wrong does not permit us to do wrong, even if we do wrong to them. This also follows from *L*: if A wrongly harms B, it is not permissible for the relevantly similar C to wrongly harm the relevantly similar D (even if D and A are one and the same). Since morality is legislative, and actions count, to wrongly harm A would be to condone A's similar harm to B. Admittedly, what it would be permissible (or even morally required) to do to gossips, criminals, or terrorists might change as a result of what they have done; namely, they might deserve condemnation or punishment. Even so, there are still things that we are not permitted to do to them, and if we do such things they *can* complain.

There must be some limits to the derogatory remarks we can make about gossips. We can neither acquiesce when sex-offenders are raped in prison, nor can we condone random, cruel, or unusual punishments being inflicted upon violent offenders. Likewise, when governments counter terrorist activity by actions that involve the loss (even if unintended) of innocent lives, this is a source for profound moral concern. The view that there are no limits on what we may say about gossips, or that everything is permitted in the struggle against crime or terrorism, is not morally acceptable. If such principles and constraints are breached, moral complaint is justified.

Moreover, something further, beyond the ubiquity of principles and constraints, is going on here and makes wronging gossips, criminals, and terrorists unacceptable. Consider a criminal who is put in prison as punishment for persistent severely violent behavior, and is then severely beaten by some prison guards, without justification. Perhaps, as we saw, it is dubious of the prisoner to feel that he can morally complain, but this is not our

Saul Smilansky

present concern. Despite the dubiousness of that complaint, it nevertheless seems that the prison guards cannot behave as they have. Note that, according to *L*, by doing so *they* would legitimize unjust severe violence.

We have, then, two contradictory views of complaint (and two interpretations of *L*). Both have considerable intuitive support. Prescriptive universal moral legislation invites two contradictory but compelling interpretations with respect to complaint: namely, that wrongdoers cannot complain when treated as they have legislated, and that wrongdoers can complain if wronged according to universal moral standards. Note that we could not easily solve the problem by rejecting *L*. *L* is an intuitively very strong principle. Moreover, as we have seen, even if we bracket *L*, both *U* and *N* are intuitively compelling in themselves. The contradiction remains. What are we to make of this?

One option is to attempt to reject one of the interpretations. Diehard absolutists can insist upon such a strong notion of human rights that it would automatically triumph over the dubiousness of any wrongdoer's complaint, dubiousness which would be shrugged off. Perhaps the wrongdoer condemns himself by complaining, or we might feel contempt for him when he complains, but he can still do so. When he does wrong then he is at fault, but when he complains he is in the right. Or, by contrast, by making the question of complaint elementary, one could deny gossips, criminals, or terrorists any opening, arguing that through their actions they have forfeited any basis for complaint, no matter how they might be treated. If we follow their implicit moral legislation, which is the moral grounding for their complaint according to this interpretation, they can have no basis for complaint. As John Rawls put it, "A person's right to complain is limited to violations of principles he acknowledges himself" (2000: 190). But I think that the intuitive salience of *both* intuitions – roughly, that what you do matters greatly to your right to complain, and that certain standards seem to allow universal complaint – should be respected, and that we should resist both of the easy ways out of the dilemma. There are perhaps examples where only one side of the antinomy will seem acceptable, but most of the moral field will not make life so easy for us.

A different option is to acknowledge that some gossips, criminals, or terrorists may put forward *particular* claims without self-contradiction, or even inconsistency. An extreme version of this would be to claim that one or one's group are superior beings, and hence need not bow before the obligation to follow the same moral principles as others. One may kill one's enemies because they are subhuman, or infidels, for instance, but the enemies may not kill one. But such claims are less interesting for us. More significantly, some gossips, criminals, and terrorists may accept the rule, but claim that they are exceptions. Because of, say, their unusual or deprived childhood, their gossiping or criminal behavior needs to be excused. Or there are particular and very extreme conditions that justify the terrorist's taking innocent lives, while harm to innocent people as a consequence of counter-terrorist activity lacks such justification. Such "special pleading" is difficult to defend in a way that will seem reasonable to the impartial (let alone to the victims), by contrast to following a wide general rule that is assumed to apply to everyone. The chances of being convincing would usually be similar to those of a person who complains about the recent infidelity of his or her spouse, which follows upon his or her own long-time infidelity, but says that "this is completely different." But, in any case, gossips, criminals, and terrorists do not typically argue in this way. Gossips feel unjustly persecuted by those who talk about them behind their back, criminals call upon the police to restrain itself and to follow the law, and terrorists demand that counter-terrorist forces follow international law and respect the sanctity of the moral innocence of civilians, all as a matter of principle. Such people typically make these complaints in wide and general terms, basing them upon universal moral and legal principles, without bothering to excuse themselves.

A third option would be to interpret such moral complaints in a way that does not imply that the complainers accept the moral principles that underlie the complaint. It is, after all, open to

Saul Smilansky

anyone to argue against a person that that person is not standing up to his or her own standards. But such a charge of moral laxity, or of hypocrisy, still does not enable us to overcome the difficulty with the sort of moral complaint we have been discussing, which must assume common moral ground. The complaints of the gossips, criminals, and terrorists assume that *they* have a moral claim, and this needs to be based upon principles they agree with. The difficulty arises precisely because they themselves manifestly do not follow those principles.

A fourth option "unmasks" the complainers: gossips, criminals, terrorists, and their possible supporters do not really believe in the standards of privacy, justice, fairness, innocence, and the sanctity of life, but rather employ these notions as mere empty rhetorical posturing. No doubt much of that also goes on. After all, it is clearly in the interests of gossips, criminals, and terrorists that they, and those they care about, not be treated in the same way as they treat others. And yet it does not seem plausible to attribute to mere self-serving cynicism all complaint that appeals to such principles. In any case, the question whether complaint is morally tenable remains.

To the extent that each of these four options is an attempt to blur the conflicting implications that we have drawn, they fail. Once we set these options aside, the contradiction between N and U still confronts us as compelling but contrasting ways of viewing moral complaints.

We need to:

1   Conclude that our intuitive views about moral complaint (N and U) are deeply contradictory. This is theoretically and practically disconcerting.

There is one further alternative:

2   Disconnect moral complaint from moral constraint.

Opting for (2) would allow us to integrate some of the insights of both N and U: namely, to say that wrongdoers cannot complain if they are treated in the ways that they have normatively supported through their actions, but that nevertheless there are constraints on how anyone may be treated. In this new option the "right" to complain may be curtailed, even when people become the target of morally wrong acts, but the general constraints on what it is morally permitted to do to other people would remain in force. So we would be affirming N on complaint, but neutralizing the major concern of the supporter of U, the worry that if a person cannot complain then he ceases to have moral protection.

It is important to see, however, that two strong commonsense assumptions are thereby abandoned: namely, that if wronged one can complain, and that if one cannot complain about an act done to one, then presumably that act may be done to one.

Going in the direction of (2) would involve the rejection of T:

T The principle of the transfer of complaint.

If it is morally impermissible to treat E in a certain way, then E has grounds for complaint if anyone treats E in that way.

Therefore (2) is also clearly unattractive, since rejecting T would mean that it may be impermissible to treat E in a certain way, but if this is done he nevertheless cannot complain! Moreover, certain people would be able to complain about a certain morally wrong act while others would not be able to complain about the very same act. Consider a situation in which E is a terrorist. He is captured, and he and his family are then severely beaten in a way that is clearly morally illegitimate. Assume that E's family opposes his terrorist ways. Then they could morally complain about the morally wrong way in which both he and they were treated, while E could complain of neither. This, beyond its distinct oddness, would again put us in tension with the universal moral intuitions lying behind L.

In cases such as those of the gossip, criminal, and terrorist, two opposing views on complaint seem compelling. In light of this contradiction between N and U, we might be attracted by the rejection of T, and try to separate constraint from complaint. But T is a strongly intuitive principle as well. Even if it does not always apply, to reject it systematically would be very unattractive. Its systematic rejection, and what this would imply, seem merely to change the paradoxicality rather than to remove it.

The Paradox of Moral Complaint seems to point to an inherent difficulty in our reflective moral intuitions. Given the legislative nature of moral agency, the plausible limitations upon reasonable moral complaint seem to contradict the inviolability of central moral constraints and the complaints that they allow. In the cases I have discussed, morality seems both to deny the possibility of moral complaint, and to insist upon its necessity.

99

10 Preferring Not to Have Been Born

A mortal, born of woman, few of days and full of trouble, comes up like a flower and withers, flees like a shadow and does not last.

Job 14: 1

100   Consider a paragraph appearing in Bernard Williams's interesting essay, "Resenting One's Own Existence," and in particular the second part of the first sentence:

> I see no way of denying that one who resents his own existence prefers that he should not have existed; and no way of interpreting that preference except in terms of thinking that one's life is not worth living. Certainly the wish not to have been born, Job's wish, is not incoherent; equally, there is no way of understanding it except from inside the actual life, and from inside the life, it surely cannot involve less than the thought that life is not worth living. (Williams 1995: 228)

I read this paragraph when I was preoccupied with thoughts about life, old age, and death, because my father was then ill with cancer from which he would later die. The relevant statement struck me as unobvious. My aim is not to consider Williams's paper but to take off from these brief remarks in a different direction. My debt to Williams's philosophizing, both in its content and in its spirit, should be obvious. I wish to cast

Saul Smilansky

doubt on his assimilating the preference for not having been born, understood as a preference for non-existence, with an evaluation that one's life is not worth living. Although the idea sounds paradoxical, there is conceptual and psychological room for the thought that one would prefer not to have been born, while at the same time believing that one's life is worth living. I want to show that the two can be prised apart. This should also help us in the general "loosening up" of seemingly obvious assumptions about these topics. And, what better way of thinking about life than to consider not having been born?

Unless otherwise specified, when speaking of non-existence I will speak of never existing rather than of dying. While speaking of (not) having been born, I shall not presuppose that persons begin to exist only at birth. Like Williams, I speak of subjective preferences and evaluations, and I make no attempt here to evaluate objectively whether life "as such," or any particular life, is worth living. In this sense all of the discussion is "internalist," without considering the judgments of others. Likewise, I concentrate on a person's own preferences and bracket the preferences that her relatives, for example, might have for her existence or non-existence.

It is difficult to think clearly about one's non-existence, for one tends (incoherently) to see the situation as though one actually hovers somewhere in the background, looking upon a situation in which one does not exist. An obvious difference between non-existence and the state of being alive and having preferences or evaluations is that in the first one does not exist. I believe that thinking attentively about that assertion would quickly induce skepticism about Williams's position. Non-existence is a state in which one does not reflect upon whether one's life is or is not worth living, nor upon any other matter. Its nature makes it altogether different from any state of one's being when one exists. This does not mean going to the opposite extreme by saying that the states are incommensurable, or even that non-existence cannot be evaluated, as some have argued (e.g., Heyd 1992: ch. 3). Despite the thin philosophical air surrounding these questions, and the seeming paradoxicality, we can still think about non-existence. It is odd to consider what not having been born would be for one, and this oddity is relevant to some "wrongful life" cases (where people have sued parents or doctors for allowing them to have been born with handicaps or diseases), and to other perplexities discussed by Williams (1973a), Parfit (1984: part 4), Heyd (1992: ch. 3), and others. But I find no similar difficulty with the idea of a life "not worth living': like Feinberg (1992: pp. 16–17), I find it natural to say that, compared with a continuously awful life, non-existence is preferable. So does Williams, it seems. My point here is that existence and non-existence are "qualitatively" so different that, as we shall see, a preference for non-existence can trump even a positive answer that comes up when it is asked what is worthwhile from within a life.

If a person said that life for her has always been happy, combining continuous satisfaction, deep self-fulfillment, and periods of ecstatic joy, but that nevertheless it would have been better not to have been born, we would find it difficult to make sense of her statement (although this is possible according to certain Far Eastern belief systems; we shall not be concerned here with their assumptions). With less extravagant but nevertheless positive estimates of the value of one's life, it does not seem incoherent to say that one would prefer not to have been born. One imbued with utilitarian ways of reflection might be at a loss to make sense of this view. If the overall balance within the life is positive, how could less than that, which non-existence presumably is, be better? But this may just show the limitations of utilitarianism, and could hardly be Williams's way of thinking (and it would in any case be misleading to consider matters here in the overly moralistic framework of utilitarianism). I see no difficulty in conceiving of the state of mind in which life is felt to be not too bad, above the line of not being worth living, but nevertheless it is felt that not having been in the whole "business" of living might not have been such a loss either, or might even have been preferable. The daily practice of living is sufferable, but it is not fulfilling. Or, taking a broader perspective upon life, it simply does not seem to have meaning for one. One may not feel that it is particularly bad to be alive, yet also not feel that one is particularly lucky to have been born. A degree of *indifference* or *ambiguity*, then, can allow for the situation I discuss: a preference for non-existence that is not coupled with an evaluation that life is not worth living.

Very different types of persons might be in such a state. Someone might have a timid nature, be ill at ease with life, apprehensive of what it holds for him. Life is not unworthy, but it is full of anxiety and so a burden nevertheless. Not to have been thrown into it might be an attractive thought. A passive person, with a chronic tiredness of life, a life-weariness, might also wish not to have existed, to have been spared both life and the need to sustain (or end) it, but nevertheless the person is not actively suffering or suicidal. By contrast, a cold, stoical person indifferent about life through an "unemotional," rationalistic way of looking upon things, is unlike the foregoing persons. Life is not very hard for her to bear, but she cannot see anything exciting in it, and the "cleanliness" or "perfection" of the thought of non-existence seems preferable. We could add various further ingredients to combine into diverse personalities. The variety of psychological types that might have a preference for non-existence without an evaluation that life is not worthwhile, living within the "bandwidth of some indifference," further strengthens my case.

The mixed nature of life, the fact that it contains a mixture of good and bad, might also lie behind a preference for non-existence. Such a state of mind may well not involve a measure of indifference as it did for the previous persons: it might even be passionate. In non-existence there is neither bad nor good. When one exists, there might be sufficiently more or greater good in one's life to force one to judge that life is worth living overall, but such a life might still include much that is bad. Note also that a preponderance of good over bad may follow from very little of each, but also from a life full of both. The bad might not overcome the good, but it could sometimes be awful, and not be erased by the good.

Consider a Holocaust survivor of the concentration camps. Such a person, reflecting upon his life near its end, upon the wife and children who were his family after the war, and on his life's work, may feel that his life was worthwhile. He might resent anyone's implying otherwise. But when he remembers the awful years of the war, his physical and psychological suffering, the loss of his first wife and child and of all his other relatives and friends, he may also think that having been spared the suffering, in not having been born, might have been preferable.

Skeptics might think that our understanding of why the Holocaust survivor might prefer not to have been born comes from sources that render the example unable to support my case, for example, myopia induced by the extremity of the suffering in question. But this need not be so. The person might have built a good life for himself, which he finds well worth living. His postwar family life in itself might even be just as good as his earlier one, and it has lasted longer. The enormity of the price, for him, might still make him prefer, on reflection (and even taking the overall view), to have been spared both the good and the bad. The goodness of his life before the Holocaust (or even after it) might just enhance, for him, the enormity of the loss, and strengthen the attraction of the thought of not having undergone any of it.

There is another kind of case that the Holocaust victim might be thought to belong to. A person can rationally prefer never to have existed and yet prefer to continue to exist. This would be rational if the person has lived through awful suffering that cannot be compensated for by his future life, but which promises nevertheless to be worth living from now on. His life as a whole wouldn't be worth living, even though his future would be. This explains how it could be rational for him at this point in his life to wish that he had never existed even though rationally he wants to go on living. But the claim I wish to defend is stronger, and applies to a preference not to have existed coupled with an evaluation that one's life as a whole has been worth living. My claim is that joy and happiness on the one hand, and suffering on the other hand, may not cancel out. They are not like monetary income and expense, which can be "added up" and only the net sum matters. In the case of suffering and

Saul Smilansky

happiness it may be plausibly suggested that in spite of the happiness being greater, it does not "cancel out" the suffering. Thus one might say of a certain life that it is worthwhile as a whole, in the sense that there is more that is positive than negative, but still that non-existence would have been preferable. The enormity of the suffering may in itself defeat the overall balance, although this balance is positive, thus inducing the thought that not having existed in the first place would have been best.

In Fortunate Misfortune we saw that, if a person prefers the overall, "favorable balance" situation, even at the price of the suffering and hardship that is part of it, then the status of that suffering and hardship may change. But one may refuse to accept the price, both in Fortunate Misfortune and here.

This "remnant" of suffering, within a life of many good experiences, reminds us of another central feature of Williams's thinking: his rejection of views that too easily dismiss the possibility for moral remnants in moral dilemmas (e.g., 1973a). One way of trying to understand what is going on here would be to construe it in temporal terms: at time t the survivor feels one way about life, at time t' he feels differently. But to do so would be to misrepresent the case. Both sentiments exist together, exerting a different pull. It is this that creates a situation whereby the actual life is worthwhile but not having had to live it is also attractive. It might be thought that, if the good outweighs the bad, then it would be irrational to prefer to have neither, over having both. But this shows, it seems to me, that such a view of rationality is inadequate. Certain analogies that we shall examine later in this chapter will further help us to see this. The appeal of the absence of the extremes of such horrible suffering and loss as the Holocaust victim had confronted cannot be dismissed as irrational, even if there is also a greater deal of good in the rest of his life – indeed, even if he has experienced his life as having enormous value. Trying to imagine what such horrors amount to would in part be to see that they are such as to make a reasonable person capable of wishing that he or she had never been born, even though his or her life has been good.

Preferring Not to Have Been Born

A third, and again very different, way in which we may understand the possibility that one can hold a preference for non-existence and yet not conclude that life is not worth living is by way of a deep dislike of oneself. One may feel oneself unworthy, see one's existence as unnecessary, or even hold oneself to be despicable: it would be best not to have been born. For all that, one might not be able to say that now, when one already exists, life is not worth living for one. There might be no overwhelming reason for one to kill oneself. The experiential quality of life is not terrible. But one resents one's existence, preferring not to have been born.

There might be external standards of evaluation behind such a state of mind: a child molester, for example, who knows that what he is doing is bad, accepts that his existence is worse than his non-existence according to a standard he appreciates, but nevertheless finds his life worthwhile. He cannot respect himself, and he prefers not to have been born, but life is liveable. Life is not worthless for him, yet in another sense life is worse than worthless; he thinks that he does not deserve to live. There is nothing paradoxical about realizing that while one's life has been good for oneself, many others have suffered as a result of one's existence, and thus (accepting the moral point of view) preferring not to have existed. But even without accepting such moral reasons, we can understand this peculiar state. One simply dislikes oneself so much that one would prefer not to have existed; one perhaps has a quasi-aesthetic distaste for being who one is. This distaste might be accompanied by a feeling that those central features of oneself that one abhors *are* oneself; that there is moreover no hope of changing into a person that one likes more. But since one was simply confronted with life, one makes the most of it, and cannot say that living is not worthwhile.

These three very different types of possible motivation can lie behind a preference for non-existence that is not coupled with an evaluation that life is not worth living. The dialectical situation is different in each of them. In the "indifference" type of case, the explanation lies primarily with the weakness of the evaluation. Since life is only just barely worth living, there is room for a preference not to have been born, the preference having arisen from anxiety, tiredness, or a fastidious "perfectionism." In the "suffering" type of case there is, by contrast, a firm positive evaluation of life as worth living, but there is also a strong contrary attraction to the thought of non-existence because non-existence lacks suffering. In the third, "self-dislike" type of case, one recognizes that one's non-existence would be preferable according to a standard that one accepts, which makes one's existence (with all of its pleasures) distasteful to one.

It is important to see that both the preference for non-existence and the evaluation of worth are distinct, and that each can be unequivocal. In many of the cases that we have explored, the preference is unambiguous. Likewise, persons need not evaluate their lives as in some ways worthwhile and in other ways not worthwhile, this being the source of the discrepancy between the preference for non-existence and the (apparent) evaluation that life is worth living. Rather, the preference for non-existence is an all-things-considered one. Nor are we talking here about fleeting, temporary preferences. There would be nothing paradoxical about having a fleeting, irrational, in-one-respect preference for something not to exist even if one considers it valuable. Finally, one could of course define the evaluation that life is not worth living as simply one kind of reply to the question of whether one prefers to have been born, but this move would only blur matters, and it lacks intrinsic motivation in the issue I am considering. This completes my argument that one can prefer not to have been born and at the same time not believe that one's life is not worth living.

It may be argued that I have missed something crucial behind Williams's position. Referring to the preference for non-existence, Williams says that "there is no way of understanding it except from inside the actual life." It is not clear to me why Williams sees this as conclusively disproving the possibility of a preference for non-existence not joined by a firm evaluation that life is not worth living. Clearly, one who has that preference must have it from within her life, for she must exist somewhere. In this sense it is a truism that any judgment must be "from inside the actual life." This cannot be all that Williams means. More importantly, a man's actual life will give content to his reflections on what would not be there for him to experience and achieve if he did not exist. In this second sense of "within," the preference for non-existence is informed by one's life. But I think I have shown how the preference for non-existence we are considering *can* exist internally in this sense, how one can have the preference when reflecting on one's actual life, aware of the potential loss.

However, there is a third important sense of "within," to which perhaps Williams was pointing. In this third sense it is more difficult to say from "within" a life that it is not worthwhile than to say it from the perspective that internalizes the thought of how things would be if one had not been born. The reason it is more difficult is simply that one cannot understand this last situation. In this sense, if one is alive one is "trapped." Saying of one's current life, as it is, that one would prefer not to have been born into it might be claimed to imply, for instance, that it was not sufficiently worthwhile for one to have brought one's children into being. However, if one had not been born one would of course not feel the loss of not having those children; the loss appears stronger just because both one, and one's children, do exist. This can be seen even in the less radical time-frame (or existence-frame) that concerns one's regret over children that one did not have. If one had had other children, then normally it would not be so easy in the emotional sense to think of not having them, but it is insane to mourn all the children that one could have had but didn't. It is also scarcely coherent: if one is liberal with one's conditionals, the number of different offspring that one did not have but could in some sense have had would be as good as infinite. If Williams means that we cannot take the "external" perspective in this sense – that one cannot conceive of the loss of one's experiential life if one had not been born as not involving the actual experience of loss of what one has in one's actual life – this seems to me simply false. One *can* think of the world as eternally empty of one, and not only as being emptied (or felt to be empty) of one. Indeed, this may be the attraction of the preference for non-existence. I see no reason to believe that people are incapable of the sort of hypothetical-logical thinking that this would involve, and that we are capable only of concrete-psychological thinking. We can evaluate whether our life, as it is, is worth living, making contact with our within-life emotions, and we can conclude that it is worth living. But we can also take an overall, more detached, view of our existence, understand what not existing means, and prefer it. The possibility of entering such a reflective perspective allows for the case I am arguing (see also Benatar 2006).

Let us consider a few analogies. Consider suicide: a woman might judge her life not to be worth living and yet not wish to kill herself. Here one could also say that if she is serious in her judgment, then, setting aside certain matters such as obligations to dependants, in some sense she "must" commit suicide. I trust that the crudity of such a view will be readily admitted. She can hardly mind very much if her not very worthwhile life ends quickly and painlessly (although even here I would not hasten to judge as irrational one who clings to life, her life, a little longer, even if she does not think that living is worthwhile: disliking being robbed of one's "not-worthwhile" life can make sense). But one can coherently be in a state that includes at one and the same time (1) seeing one's life as not worth living, (2) not minding very much whether one lives or dies, and (3) not doing anything to end one's life. There is a distance between judging one's life to be not worthwhile and ending it oneself. By analogy there is also a distance between judging one's life to be somewhat worthwhile and preferring to have been alive in the first place. There is more to the good life, to a life one prefers to have been born into, than a mere overall positive balance of well-being.

A common state of mind for many people towards the end of their lives, most often in old age, is to feel that they have had enough, that it would not be bad if their life had ended already. I do not think that we could force all such people into the straitjacket of saying that they find no meaning or pleasure in the life that still awaits them. No, they might say, it would not be bad to continue to exist a few more years, it would be fine; nevertheless it might be best if I were to die now. One immediate objection might be that further thoughts are at work here: the fear of being a burden, of being degraded, or of suffering pain at the very end of one's life. Or, differently, one might have the "perfectionist" sense that although there might be a few reasonably good years ahead, they would be nothing like the previous years, and the person would feel the comparative decline; or, the "average" quality of one's overall life would suffer (Hurka 1993: ch. 6). While such thoughts may be important, I do not think that they, or similar factors, must be present in order that the view under discussion be allowed.

One form that such reflection often takes is the preference for dying unawares, say, in one's sleep, as compared to living a longer life in slow decline during which one knows for a long period of time what is about to happen. People notoriously have contrasting preferences on this matter. Within certain limits, I have the general preference for knowing what is ahead of me. But I find no inherent difficulty in understanding someone who prefers the opposite option, even at the price of a shorter life, and I do not see her as necessarily committed to the view that the toll of such knowledge is experientially greater than the combined value of the extra period of life one could still have after being thus informed. The person may not actually make the comparison, but even if she makes it, and even if she admits that the years would be worth living, her preference then and there for dying unawares may be stronger. If I do not die unawares but keep living in gradual decline, one may think, I may occasionally appreciate that I have been given this further time, and think this period of my life worth living. And yet I may prefer to die unawares without this extra period. It is not manifestly irrational to want to die unawares even if one thereby loses in this "trade-off" a few months or even years that might be worth living. Reasons akin to those we saw with the preference for non-existence – the pointlessness in living, the salience of the bad, and self-dislike – appear when people are considering the last part of life.

Saul Smilansky

I could be accused of conflating two very different matters in the last two paragraphs: non-existence owing to not having been born, and early death. There are clearly differences here. When one prefers early death, one would usually have the thought that one has lived a worthwhile life until now, something not shared by those who have not been born (cf. Kamm 1993: part 1). However, thinking about the preference for early death helps to tease out some of our intuitions about the preference for non-existence. At the very least this discussion should be instructive in making us doubt comparative "quantitative" ways of thinking. The "acceptability" of preferences for early death (such as we have considered) cannot be denied even when much "worthwhile living time" is lost. The "option" of initial non-existence, if attractive, seems to me to involve some of the same preferences as the option for early death, notably "giving up" a period of existence when one's life would be worthwhile. In one way, the absolute nature of the "giving up" in the idea of not being born makes it even more difficult (rather than easier) to assimilate to an alleged necessity for an evaluation of life's being not worth living. The person preferring to be without the additional years in old age "gives up" something from the perspective of an evaluation from "within" a life, in the second sense noted above. The preference for not being born involves the attractiveness of a lack of such awareness and evaluation.

It is important, finally, that we see that it is not only that one may prefer not to have been born even though one's life is worth living. We can also reverse our perspective: even if one feels that it would have been better not to have been born, one can still find life worth living in various ways. Our different evaluations, as well as the relations between our evaluations and the suitability of our actions, can be reasonably pried apart more than is commonly understood.

Paradoxically, preferring not to have been born need not be a consequence of an evaluation that one's life is not worth living, nor need such a preference imply this evaluation. We explored a number of ways in which the distinctness of these ideas could be understood. We can now see how one who does not find

111

much point in life, or who finds a point but is brutalized by its hardships, or who deeply dislikes himself but nevertheless does not hold that life is "not worth living," can still prefer to have been spared the whole thing, not to have been in life from the beginning.

Saul Smilansky

A Meta-Paradox: Are Paradoxes Bad?

Problems worthy of attack prove their worth by hitting back.
Piet Hein, *Grooks*

A genuine paradox is surely a sign that something is not going well. Contradiction and absurdity are not good news. We ought to be even more displeased, perhaps (or at least displeased in a further way) when we confront a *moral* paradox, and to hope that the paradox will go away, or somehow be overcome. Moreover, we ought to try to arrange moral life so that paradoxes are avoided.

Paradoxically, this is not so. Matters are complex, yet at least within the scope of the moral paradoxes that we have investigated, we can see that we ought not always to avoid or even to mitigate paradoxes. Neither ought we to be always displeased that paradoxes occur. On the contrary, paradoxes are often a sign that things are going well, morally and personally. A paradox may be an optimistic indicator. Not infrequently, I shall argue, we should even arrange things so that matters become more paradoxical!

Paradoxes can be good or bad in various senses and in various ways: in what they imply about the world, the state of our knowledge, rationality, the general status of morality, philosophy, and so on. We shall ask questions on these issues in the concluding chapter. Here we shall focus on the more limited question, of whether it is good or bad, in the sense of making moral and personal life better or worse, that we have moral paradoxes. This question has never been asked, to the best of my knowledge. Let us begin by looking at some cases. Consider Fortunate Misfortune. In situations of Fortunate Misfortune, we recall, what seems to be a clear and great misfortune leads to good fortune. If the resulting good fortune, in the lives of the purported victims of FM, is so much better than their lives are likely to have become without the original misfortune, then it becomes unclear whether the original misfortune was indeed a misfortune.

The paradox of Fortunate Misfortune will not exist unless there is misfortune, but misfortunes will sometimes befall people. The paradox can then be avoided, but at a price: if the misfortune exists, but its victims do not overcome it as Abigail and Abraham did, then there is simply a misfortune that leads to failure, disappointment, and misery, and that is no paradox. Given that misfortune exists, it is better if it becomes fortunate: that is a triumph for people like Abigail and Abraham, and makes our world better. It is hard to see anything wrong with the fact that we end up

with a paradox. Making life a paradox, here, is an achievement; life thereby begins to make sense. The existence of a paradox is not to be regretted, but rather cheered, for it is a victory for the human spirit when a misfortune has been overcome and turned into a launching pad for good fortune. The more victories the better, even though paradoxicality increases.

The Paradox of Beneficial Retirement presents a very different situation. But here as well the paradox can be avoided: one way in which this could happen is for people not to choose occupations where what they do significantly matters, or in which special skills are required. For then they will not be confronted with the dilemma posed by the realization that if they were to leave their job, someone much better than they would probably replace them. Another way in which the paradox can be avoided is if the stream of new recruits to the profession were to dry up, for then those already inside it will have escaped the paradox – they need not think about possible replacements. But surely we do not wish people en masse to cease to have ambitions, stop pursuing their calling, and forgo the pursuit of excellence, in professions

Saul Smilansky

where what they do and how well they do it matter greatly. And we should not wish these things even if it would thereby entail people risking being confronted by the paradox themselves, or bring about this confrontation for those already inside their chosen profession. A world where everyone would aspire to no more than a job at McDonald's may be paradox-free, but at the same time a (burger-filled) nightmare. Neither the good life nor the good society lies with the elimination of the sort of moral and personal risk involved in the Paradox of Beneficial Retirement. We should aim to make the world safe for paradox.

This should not lead us into the opposite extreme: it *is* important for individuals to plan their professional careers, and perhaps the paradox needs to be considered when such planning is done ("perhaps" due to the possible benefits of ignorance, as we noted when discussing this paradox). But the salience of this paradox is also a good sign, a sign that many people are eager to be significant contributors to important professions and pursuits, and that individual excellence matters. Such patterns of personal ambition ought to be encouraged – although this increases the prevalence of the paradox. From the social perspective as well, we should not want an unlimited supply of young potential doctors, detectives, and academics knocking on the doors of their professions. But some such surplus is a good thing for a profession and those it serves, even though this builds up the paradox.

The two paradoxes about Justice and the Severity of Punishment bring up other questions and show us that matters are more complex. Since the paradoxes follow from the normative insistence that both desert and deterrence should play a central role in sentencing, we can avoid the paradoxes by opting only for one of the two. But such avoidance is a price we should not wish to pay: the paradoxical conclusion of an argument depends on its premises, but we should not wish to avoid the conclusion by ditching a true premise. In this sense it is trivially true that the existence of a paradox is better than its non-existence.

Of course, we need to apply judgment here. Once we admit the category of the "existential paradox," a paradox that is found to be absurd even after due reflection but whose truth cannot be

A Meta-Paradox: Are Paradoxes Bad?

rejected, then the fact that a set of premises leads to absurdity does not entail the automatic rejection of those premises. Recall that absurdity does not imply strict contradiction. Sometimes the absurdity is decisive (which is why the Paradox of the Baseline was a successful *reductio* of choice-egalitarianism). But in a case such as punishment, giving up either on deterrence or on desert (in the sense of accepting mitigating circumstances) is normatively unacceptable. Rather, we must live with the measure of absurdity, and tragedy, involved. To the extent that current systems of justice do not take into account the pertinent considerations (say, they do not sufficiently care about mitigation), then they are less paradoxical – but also more unjust.

Nicholas Rescher (2001) holds that paradoxes are the outcome of philosophical "over-commitment." The way to overcome paradoxes is to reduce those commitments that generate the paradoxes, not to endorse so many beliefs. I don't think that this diagnosis holds for all paradoxes; the sources of paradoxicality are varied (and we shall say more about this later). But with the two paradoxes about Justice and the Severity of Punishment, the issue of over-commitment *is* salient, relating to our insistence both on deterrence and on desert-based mitigation. Yet even here it is far from clear that what Rescher would call over-commitment ought to be given up. Perhaps it is natural to morality. At any rate, the commitment both to deterrence and to mitigation does not seem like a mistake: it is, rather, that moral reality falls short. Calling our minimally acceptable moral commitments "over-commitment" can be misleading. We ought not to give them up, even if that entails swallowing the paradoxical consequences. Giving them up would miss the lesson that we are being taught here, about the strength of paradox and absurdity in the context of punishment.

The two paradoxes about Justice and the Severity of Punishment do present us, however, with a good way of limiting paradoxicality: if we can reduce crime, then paradoxicality in sentencing will also become less common. Another prima facie good way of achieving a reduction of paradoxicality might be narrowing the gaps between the "privileged" and the "under-

Saul Smilansky

privileged." A bad way would be catching fewer criminals. All this shows that the idea of avoiding paradox has a lot to be said for it. In fact, as far as I can see there is nothing good about *this* paradox. Which only goes to emphasize the oddness when we discover that the opposite is also often the case, namely, that in some contexts paradoxes ought to be welcomed and even encouraged.

We do not have to look far for the potential goodness of paradoxicality: the topic of the severity of punishment brings us also the Paradox of Non-Punishment. One horn of the antinomy in Non-Punishment asks how we can reject the temptation of succeeding in deterrence even without the need to have recourse to actual punishment. But to fall for the temptation and take up the proposal to threaten with overpunishment (even to accept it in theory, let alone in practice) is also to embrace, and enhance, paradoxicality. In other words, it amounts to declaring that a certain morally paradoxical state is so preferable, overall, that we wish to bring it about intentionally.

The Paradox of the Baseline pertains only to choice-egalitarianism, and its effect on it is destructive. Here the paradox indeed needs to be avoided; and we can do so by not opting for choice-egalitarianism. The paradox forces us to rethink the premises. But this is atypical among our paradoxes. As we have already begun to see, most of the paradoxes cannot be overcome in this way.

In the class of paradoxes that are to be welcomed lies also Morality and Moral Worth. The reduction of suffering and grievous wrongs is a moral gain, and ought to be cheered and supported. True, this gain also threatens the achievement of the highest forms of moral value. But this byproduct cannot be permitted to change our basically positive view of the reduction of suffering and grievous wrongs.

It is interesting to see how thoroughly the paradox of Morality and Moral Worth tracks moral improvement. The paradoxes of punishment obviously depend on the existence of crime, and would happily disappear were everyone law-abiding and moral without the threat of punishment. Even the salience of the

Paradox of Moral Complaint would decline if people became more moral. In Morality and Moral Worth matters go in the opposite direction: moral improvement might altogether eliminate the demand for the heights of moral worth. In a morally perfect world there is no need for high moral worth. The good is absurd. The further the moral improvement, the greater the paradoxicality. Goodness and paradoxicality here go hand in hand in the most fundamental way.

The paradoxicality hence brings to the fore ambiguity, even when the correct judgment is clear: we see here, as we did with other paradoxes, that gain involves loss (as well as that loss can involve gain). The very fact that there is something important to mourn in the elimination of suffering and grievous wrongs shows the paradoxicality. Such ambiguity comes up often in Not Being Sorry about the Morally Bad. We may wish that we lived in a world in which people did not succeed through the misfortune of others. But such a world is unreal: wherever there is competition, whether it is for the love of others or for their business, or even for the opportunity to increase learning or beauty in the world, there will be those who do less well. This "at the expense of" feature of social and emotional life would be intolerable were it not permissible *not* to be sorry when bad things happen to others. There is an interesting question concerning the degree to which we wish our world to be competitive, but any realistic model would leave room for the legitimate absence of sorrow (at least in the form of sorrow *that*) at the misfortune of others, an absence of sorrow on which depends our ability to function successfully and happily.

This becomes even clearer if we consider the second context in which it is possible not to be sorry, or even to be happy, when bad things happen to others, namely, when bad people (racists, rapists, and so on) are harmed beyond what they deserve. Surely, as the Bible has warned us, there could be too much happiness at the fall of one's enemy. But the present point is that we need to tolerate some of it. Again, as with competition, tolerating people's natural human sensibilities implies that we need to tolerate paradox. Here we would perhaps not wish to go so far as to say that the existence of paradoxicality is a good sign, but we need not see it as bad.

None of the above shows that paradoxicality is in itself good, or that we should not typically perceive it as a price. But as we have seen, paradoxicality can sometimes be viewed favorably for a number of reasons: as a mark of good things, as a (sometimes harmless) byproduct of good things, as something that we ought to aim for in order to produce the good, and, finally, in some cases perhaps even as part of the essence of the good. I do not think that we ought to enhance paradoxicality for its own sake. Admittedly, that might add color and variety to the world. But we must not forget that we are speaking here about morality. Making moral life more absurd is not, in itself, an acceptable aim. There is already more than enough absurdity around.

We might deepen our understanding why moral paradoxes cannot be simply solved, and need not be bad, if we reflect on the question "Where do paradoxes come from?" In some cases, unusual situations make commonsense assumptions ("a misfortune is unfortunate"; "if a person considers his life worth living, he is glad to have been born") false, or at least questionable, in a way that generates a paradox. Sometimes it is widely prevalent situations that do the work, rather than unusual ones: for example, the fact that the category of persons who are deserving of lesser punishment will be the same category as those who will typically be deterred only through greater punishment. Or, the paradox may simply emerge from the thought that we might arrange things more successfully (as the common assumption that "a justice system cannot threaten with unjust punishment" is questioned in Non-Punishment). The origins of a paradox like Not Being Sorry are again very different, since it is based on the emotional-normative limits of what we can expect even of the moral person. With Beneficial Retirement, by contrast, the expectation from many people is greater than we have previously recognized, primarily due to the surprising way in which the notion of integrity operates in that context. Moral Complaint emerges both from the nature of central moral concepts and from our basic moral intuitions, which generate two contrastive positions on complaint. I shall not go over the sources of all the paradoxes.

There is, then, great variety here. Paradoxes can emerge from stubborn facts, whether usual or unusual. They can also emerge from new ways of thinking; from the reasonable limitations of our moral emotions; from the way our moral concepts work; and from central moral intuitions. One of the things that the notion of the "existential paradox" helps us see is that moral paradoxes are ingrained in morality, and probably cannot be completely overcome. The desire to avoid moral paradoxes may take us away from morality. Some moral paradoxes, moreover, derive from contexts of social and moral progress, as we have seen. In any case, the paradoxes seem to come out more as we become more aware of pertinent facts, distinctions, concepts, and intuitions. As our understanding increases, so does our awareness of paradoxicality, and of its deep and entrenched nature.

It is interesting to contemplate what it would mean to live in a moral world where a great deal more – or perhaps even everything – would be paradoxical. That would hardly be something to look forward to. But a measure of paradoxicality, in certain locations within our moral universe, surprisingly turns out to be a good thing. It is sometimes better to have the "messiness" of paradox than moral clarity without paradox.

The ideal of an ethical system or worldview that is simple, comprehensive, and systematic is philosophically attractive. And everyone should share the hope that moral life makes good sense. Both ideal and hope are put under strain by the existence of moral paradoxes; this will be taken up in the concluding chapter. I do not wish to encourage complacency about the existence of moral paradoxes, not only because to be blind to the philosophical ideal and impervious to the human hope would not be admirable. As we saw in the example of punishment, it *is* often good to aim to reduce paradoxicality. Frequently, however, this is not the case, which creates the present meta-paradox. It is natural to think that moral paradoxes indicate that things are bad, like a torn blanket that leaves us exposed. But this

Saul Smilansky

metaphor can be turned around: the moral blanket may cover more because it is made of the stuff of paradox. It seems that we need to get used not only to the existence of numerous moral paradoxes, but to the realization that sometimes this is a good thing, so that we actually need to be happy about paradoxes, and try to increase the paradoxicality.

A Meta-Paradox: Are Paradoxes Bad?

12 Reflections on Moral Paradox

Wellness lies in the capacity to straddle paradoxes within the self. Creativity lies in the fresh negotiations of paradox within the self as well as between the self and the material and relational outside world.

Stuart A. Pizer, *Building Bridges: The Negotiation of Paradox in Psychoanalysis*

Reaching the end of a book filled with moral paradoxes might be compared to completing a "survival" course that instructs people in the skills needed to face physical danger and adversity. We have taken unforeseen turns, walked on treacherous ground that we had thought we knew, and confronted unfamiliar beasts, hidden traps, and dangerous dilemmas. New problems posed novel challenges, threatening familiar assumptions, well-proven principles, and commonsense habits of thought. What we came in with simply was not good enough, and we had to make do as we went along. Until the end we could not feel at ease, and nightmares may persist. Why bother? For the quality of the experience, for the self-knowledge gained, and to prepare for things to come.

These philosophical paradoxes raise issues that we morally and personally need to attend to. Moral paradoxes show that doing moral philosophy can be fun, but they also bring up disquieting problems. They can make us wiser and not only in the Socratic sense of discovering that we do not know.

Saul Smilansky

Some of the paradoxes take up familiar topics (punishment, equality, universality), and say new things about them. Other paradoxes take up questions that in themselves have rarely, if ever, been posed: When is a bad occurrence a misfortune? When ought one to retire? Can one prefer not to have been born, even though one considers one's life worth living? May one be happy that morally bad things happen to others? More generally, we have learned that paradoxes can be "existential," whereby the "fault" lies not with the premises or argumentation, but in moral and personal reality, which just *is* paradoxical. The paradox itself is not a mistake, it reveals absurdity. Another discovery was that moral paradoxes can be good, and that paradoxicality might need to be encouraged. In this concluding chapter I shall first briefly review some landmarks in our journey to the individual paradoxes, and then proceed to reflect more broadly on what we can learn from this journey.

Paradoxes of antinomy occur, we recall, when two sets of beliefs have strong support but contradict each other. We cannot see a way of giving up either, but neither can we hold on to both. Cases of Fortunate Misfortune invite the response that, once we understand matters we see clearly that there has not been a misfortune, *and* that of course there has been one. The Paradox of Non-Punishment presents the irresistible temptation of achieving through the justice system (within a certain sphere) zero crime together with zero punishment, together with the manifest unacceptability of the proposal. In the Paradox of Moral Complaint, we are at once attracted by the idea that people in certain situations cannot morally complain but also by the idea that it must be possible for them to do so. And both conclusions seem to derive from the same principle. The Paradox of Beneficial Retirement also starts out in this form: surely p, but irresistibly not-p. In the end, however, this paradox may belong in the veridical camp, without losing its status as a genuine paradox, for the seemingly absurd case for unwanted retirement is arguably dominant (in veridical paradoxes, we recall, a seemingly absurd result is shown to be true). Similarly veridical are Preferring Not to Have Been Born (the idea that one might prefer not to have been born although one finds life worth living), and On Not Being Sorry about the Morally Bad (the initially very implausible idea that one can be moral but nevertheless be not sorry, or even be happy, about the occurrence of the morally bad).

With the two paradoxes of Justice and the Severity of Punishment, the relevant beliefs and values (deterrence and desert-based mitigation) oppose one another, but the "fault" seems to be in reality. "That is life," we might say, "life just *is* paradoxical." The paradox seems to be existential. With blackmail, it is the reply as to why we single out blackmail for moral condemnation (there is nothing good about it) that (perhaps) we find the most paradoxical. So there seems to be a solution to the puzzling status of blackmail, but this solution is paradoxical. We can interpret matters here as involving an unacceptable paradoxicality such that we cannot rest until we have ridden ourselves of, or as existential, namely, we need to accept it and live with it. I favor the latter interpretation. Once again, unless we find a different solution we have to resign ourselves to the paradoxicality. With Morality and Moral Worth we know that the paradox is existential and that there is no solution, because the paradoxicality emerges when things are good, and grows when they improve. Morally, we cannot rid ourselves of the paradoxicality. The good and the absurd become inseparable.

The Paradox of the Baseline explicitly brings out a feature of many of these paradoxes: that different ways of presenting the paradoxicality are possible. We can explain what is going on as an instance of the antinomy type of paradox (on the one hand, the Non-Effectives ought to get a "top" baseline income and join Bill Gates, but on the other hand they also cannot be placed at such a huge advantage over the Effectives; and no solution seems capable of satisfying both demands). We can also see that a difficulty lies in the very fact that a position that places such high positive value on choice can then penalize choice so dramatically. But perhaps the paradox is best understood if we see it as *a reductio* of choice-egalitarianism: even if we are attracted by the idea that no one may fare better than another through no fault or choice of his or her own, most of us will be horrified to

Saul Smilansky

discover what this entails. Choice-egalitarianism yields, as it were, a falsidical paradox. Something basic in the egalitarian assumptions needs to be revised. The fact that the paradoxicality can be elucidated in alternative ways teaches us again about the limits of trying to constrain the notion of "paradox" into an overly narrow definition. Paradoxes are diverse, wild things that resist being pinned down.

Most of the paradoxes we have examined lie well within the traditional fold of paradoxes. Ethicists need not feel that applying the term "paradox" to the problems they deal with would be inappropriate. The antinomy Paradox of Moral Complaint, for instance, is no less a paradox than many paradoxes of antinomy prevailing elsewhere in philosophy. Fortunate Misfortune or the Paradox of Non-Punishment present us with the same sort of dizzying reversals of reflection and intuition (as well as the "Wow" feeling) as many classical paradoxes. Nor was there a shortage of veridical paradoxes in the seemingly absurd but well-supported conclusions that I have presented. Moral paradoxes naturally differ from other paradoxes, but such differences mirror the familiar differences between normative and non-normative reasoning, reflecting the different natures of the pertinent concepts.

One of the familiar features of the older non-moral paradoxes is a self-erasing aspect. The classic example is the "liar paradox," where by saying "I am lying" the speaker invites the thought that if he is indeed lying, then he tells the truth, and then he isn't lying. This feature is broadly exhibited, in various ways (causal, logical), by a number of the moral paradoxes. In Fortunate Misfortune, the misfortune transforms itself into good fortune because it is a misfortune. But is it then still a misfortune? In Non-Punishment, the very threat of radically severe and unjust punishment vitiates the need for any punishment and injustice. And in Moral Complaint, both the wrongdoer who complains and those who wrong him have undermined their own stances. Further comparisons between moral and non-moral paradoxes lie beyond the scope of our inquiry.

What is the connection between the moral paradoxes and skepticism? This is not an easy question. Obviously the paradoxes deal with (and bring out) topics in which matters are less normatively clear than in much of morality, and we investigated them in a critical and skeptical spirit. Questions tend to be better than answers in philosophy, and when the questions concern paradoxes we should not expect things to be easier. Our results encourage the thought that we should not come hastily to conclusions and ought to be doubtful of our capacities. In a world in which people are all too often attracted by facile judgments and simplistic ideologies, awareness of paradoxicality should serve as a useful antidote. Our investigations in this volume can, however, be helpful in limiting moral skepticism, not only in the lopsided way of throwing into relief the areas where paradox is minimal but in that sometimes the paradoxes or their solutions themselves seem to provide fairly clear moral conclusions (as with Blackmail, or with Moral Worth, for instance). Sometimes, indeed, it is the strength of the conclusion that makes for the paradoxicality. Making progress in charting corners of the "land of paradox" actually gives a peculiar satisfaction and can build our confidence. For, if we can make sense of things here, this surely has some positive implications for our hopes from philosophical ethics more broadly. Even when we ended up with doubts and uncertainty, this was not because we saw reason for general skepticism about truth, even truth in ethics, but due to factors such as the complexity of relevant considerations. Often the problem with morality is not that we cannot know anything, but that we seem to know too much.

By this stage, the unsettling nature of many of the paradoxes does not need pointing out. Some paradoxes are morally, personally, or socially threatening, and invite questions as to whether it would perhaps be better if people did not become aware of them (for example, Beneficial Retirement, Non-Punishment, Not Being Sorry, and Moral Complaint, for different reasons). Note that this might be so irrespective of one's view on the paradox. Other paradoxes seem more innocent. Some of the paradoxes have known solutions (Blackmail; perhaps Beneficial Retirement; perhaps Fortunate Misfortune), while others do not really require a solution, the paradoxicality simply being there in the result

Saul Smilansky

(Preferring Not to Have Been Born and Morality and Moral Worth, for example). Or so it seems. The Paradox of Moral Complaint certainly seems to call for a solution, but I am at a loss as to what it might be. The compromise "solution" I tentatively proposed, separating complaint from constraint, seems almost as dubious as the rejection of either side of the antinomy. I find the Paradox of Non-Punishment similarly begging for further work. So, concerning some of the paradoxes, it seems that we know broadly what there is to know, and that the paradox exists because that is how reality is or because of our considered conceptions, in a way that I doubt can change much. The main work waiting for us to do is to explore what this means. But I may well be wrong: with paradoxes one should always be doubtful. With other paradoxes, I have little doubt that there is room for much more to be said, and perhaps for radical revisions in our thinking as a result of them.

The existence of paradoxes led Graham Priest (e.g., 2006) to argue that contradictions can be true, and rationally believed. I shall not follow such extreme suggestions for the revision of logic itself. Some of the moral paradoxes we have explored may nevertheless suggest that the very idea of a wholly consistent and coherent moral view is impossible. Inherently, morality may need to be limited in scope or restricted to certain areas, and moral theory unavoidably incomplete, and overextended. In this way moral paradoxes should induce doubts about the nature of morality, the role of moral intuitions, and the ambitions of moral theory. But it is surely too early to tell whether our pessimism ought to be so striking, or what form it ought to take.

There seem to be a number of possibilities here: first, we might want to embrace contradiction within logic, hence there would be nothing remarkable about moral paradoxes even if they involve strict contradictions. As I said, I do not wish to follow this direction of radical logical revisionism. Second, morality may be special because it is thought that there are no truths in morality (or that paradigmatically moral claims are neither true nor false, or something of this sort). I do not want to assume such (meta-ethical) skepticism about the status of morality as such, either.

So, what options are left? One option is knowledge-based (epistemic): to say that logic cannot stand strict contradictions, and morality needs to meet logical requirements, but that the apparent contradictions indicate that we simply do not as yet sufficiently understand the paradoxes. The fault is in us. I believe that this may well be the case with some of the paradoxes (Non-Punishment, perhaps), but not with others. With the others, I believe that two things may be going on: first, that we have serious, "existential," moral absurdity, which nevertheless does not involve logical contradiction. As long as paradoxicality does not require contradiction – and this book has shown that even a demanding notion of paradox doesn't – we can have paradox with (logical and meta-ethical) impunity. We have seen that some of the paradoxes probably even have solutions – we choose one side of the antinomy – but that they nevertheless indicate paradoxicality and absurdity (Beneficial Retirement, for instance). With other paradoxes there is no contradiction, but the paradox indicates that moral reality is absurd (the two paradoxes about Justice and the Severity of Punishment, and Morality and Moral Worth, are very different examples of this type). There can in such cases be a contradiction between our psychological expectation that moral and personal reality will not be absurd, and the reality where it is, but that is not a logical problem. Does this cover everything? I am not sure. Sometimes I suspect that, with a few of the paradoxes, we may have to give up and say that, as far as we can make sense of things, some parts of morality itself may not be entirely coherent. But, once again, it is too early to tell.

It is significant that even when there seems to be a solution to a paradox, this does not generate a great deal of relief. It *is* important that (if you agree with my tentative conclusion) "It wasn't a misfortune" is the most plausible view on Fortunate Misfortune, or that, in Beneficial Retirement, retirement may be the morally and personally compelling decision. Yet the thought that either paradox therefore evaporates is mistaken. The paradox is larger than its solution. The nature of the (theoretical or practical) resolution of a paradox may, in one way, just increase our sense of paradox and awe. While a paradox arouses dissonance, if it is solved the nature of the resolution might involve further and particular paradoxicality.

Living with paradoxes, living a life that seeks to be informed by paradoxicality rather than by an effort to escape the awareness of it, requires, first, a high toleration for uncertainty. It also mandates a willingness to accept that when we do come to know what there is to know, we may still find matters paradoxical. Ignorance and knowledge may be equally difficult to live with, and (since knowledge is knowledge of paradoxes) may not even differ so much.

The major contribution of the moral paradoxes surely lies in the lessons of each. Yet, beyond the individual paradoxes, can we speak about a "paradoxical" way of doing moral philosophy? I noted in the Introduction some of the characteristics of the philosophical temperament that looks for moral paradoxes. In the end, the virtues of "the paradoxical way" will not differ much from those of any good philosophizing: the attempt at clarity, perseverance, abstract imagination, openness and tolerance of uncertainty, going where the argument leads. "Paradox hunting" will merely tend to be associated with some of these characteristics to greater degrees. It will seek the cracks in our concepts and theories, respect all seemingly relevant intuitions even when they contradict each other, expect the crooked rather than the straight path to prevail, and be particularly attuned to self-reference, antinomy, and the absurd. I hope that more paradoxically inclined moral philosophers will emerge, for in the light of what we have learned here about our moral ideas and about moral reality, such a development should be fruitful. But I certainly do not claim that this is the only right way of doing moral philosophy.

Certain topics, themes, and tendencies recur in the paradoxes that I have explored. The question how things would be if you weren't "here" plays a central role in Beneficial Retirement and, more radically, in Not Being Sorry and Preferring Not to Have Been Born. Both Fortunate Misfortune and Not Being Sorry share the idea that we may take surprisingly diverse views of bad occurrences. Not Being Sorry and Moral Complaint show the gap that can exist between morally evaluating situations as bad or wrong, and yet allowing lack of sorrow about them (Not Being Sorry), or not allowing room for complaint about them (Moral Complaint). Further investigation of the connections between these two paradoxes in particular, and of the general "lenient," self-referential, and reciprocal view of morality that they point to, should be rewarding. Moral Worth and Fortunate Misfortune investigate the bad side of "obviously" good occurrences and the good side of "obviously" bad events, respectively. Fortunate Misfortune and Preferring Not to Have Been Born bring out the role of "parts" and "wholes" in lives, and the leeway we have in deciding about their relative importance. And both Moral Complaint and Fortunate Misfortune are concerned with limiting the circumstances in which certain categories of persons may legitimately complain. Further such connections should become clearer as we continue to think about and gradually come to understand the individual paradoxes better.

Should we be troubled by the existence of paradoxes? Yes, in the sense that we need to try to solve them. A paradox may be a mere clog in the flow of our understanding. If the obstruction can be removed but we have not yet recognized that fact, we have failed to give our own understanding a fresh opportunity. We must not resign ourselves to paradoxicality without a fight, for otherwise the very realization of paradoxicality carries no conviction. Beyond that, it depends. If for all our honest efforts we end up with paradox, then that too is something that we have learned. Perhaps there is no complete escape from paradox in the sentencing of criminals (or we ought to enhance it even, by sometimes accepting the proposal made in Non-Punishment). Perhaps many people do need to confront the personal challenge of the benefits that can accrue from their own (undesired) early retirement. Perhaps, while most paradoxes uncovered hidden depths, the solution to the blackmail paradox shows that some of morality is disturbingly shallow, and that much less is going on, morally, than we thought. Perhaps we have no choice but to set forth into the morally uncharted waters of separating complaint from constraint – as implausible or distasteful as such results may seem.

Saul Smilansky

What does the accumulation of moral paradoxes teach us about moral reality and about our ethical views? What is its personal-existential import? To begin with, the prevalence of complexity and the need to be ready for surprises become apparent. "A misfortune is a misfortune" – well, surprisingly, things are not so simple. Nor, often, is the answer to the question "Can this person complain?" The fact that we have such very different paradoxes on the same topic of punishment is in itself significant. Few people have been as open, sophisticated, and sensitive in their moral reflection as Bernard Williams, but even he thought that if one prefers not to have been born then obviously one does not find life worth living. This seems to be a mistake. The natural thought that the egalitarian ideal should be choice-based makes good intuitive sense until we see that it leads into a den of paradoxes. Similarly dubious is the "obvious" inference from something's being morally bad to a conclusion that is often not the case: that morally good people can be expected not to be happy about the matter. As Albert Einstein apparently did not say, "Everything should be made as simple as possible, but not simpler."

The relationship between the paradoxes and our theories of normative ethics is complex, and uncertain. Risking over-simplification, I suggest that Blackmail brings out the primacy of utilitarian considerations, while Preferring Not to Have Been Born illustrates their crudity. Two Paradoxes about the Severity of Punishment brings out the difficulties of holding on at once to consequentialist and deontological (desert) considerations, without giving any indication that we can give up on either. The plurality of ethical theories needed in order to make sense of the morality of punishment makes matters existentially paradoxical. Not Being Sorry adds a virtue theory component, while Moral Complaint – the self-reflexive and perhaps substantially contractual nature of much of morality. On the level of theory as well, pluralism is strengthened, and seems unavoidable. And, while theory was sometimes important (as when thinking about punishment), theories were often not very helpful, and the particulars of a given paradoxical context made all the difference.

It was interesting to see how our distinctly analytical way of doing philosophy sometimes generated results more typical of Continental philosophy (such as "existential paradoxes" and the prevalence of the absurd). Some conclusions that are more familiar within Far Eastern forms of thought (such as the need for accepting unhappy situations, and the limits of rationality) were also seen to emerge.

The variety and depth of moral situations and ways in which we can view matters come forth in striking ways, which I will not reiterate. Paradoxes are not mere intellectual puzzles, but entry points that give us access to underlying philosophical structures, open up possibilities, and provide insights. They exhibit the endemic complexity of reality, the need to expect the surprising, and the prevalence of variety and depth. Moreover, reality seems unquestionably perverse. In this way the paradoxes are like black holes in our moral and personal universe, where odd things happen. The paradoxes exhibit the irrationality of life and confront us with it. The good moral intentions of the choice-egalitarians, when joined with a sensible emphasis on choice, lead them into absurdity. The fact that misfortunes often prove to be good fortunes complicates our evaluation of situations, but beyond that there is something positively perverse about many such situations, and about their implications (say, for compensation, or for remorse). The very goal of morality and the main species of moral worth turn out to proceed in opposite directions. Sometimes, the perversity brought forth by the moral paradoxes is a good thing.

The plurality of fundamental values also emerges clearly, in every paradox. Use of the word "tragic" would often not be out of place, as when we see what integrity requires in the Paradox of Beneficial Retirement, or the moral "mess" that is punishment. The paradoxes show at once the strength of our capacity for reasoning and the prevalence of unreason in reality. Indeed, by uncovering unreason we affirm our capacities for reasoning and understanding. Yet while restless reason can make genuine advances, it is likely to remain restless. The possibility that the more we understand the more paradoxical matters will appear

Saul Smilansky

cannot be ruled out. We should proceed in doing moral philosophy, but the prospects for a future morality that is fully integrated and paradox-free look dim. Paradoxicality is here to stay. Perhaps we should not regret this too much. As we saw in the meta-paradox, some paradoxicality is a good thing, and follows from positive social or personal developments. Moreover, the paradoxes also create breathing space in which human life can come forth in its richness and diversity, as well as helping us to put our abilities, our aspirations, and ourselves in perspective. Paradox seems to be inherent in morality and, indeed, in the human condition.

Openness, tolerance, carefulness, and intellectual modesty seem in any case to be necessary. With such variety, complexity, depth, and perversity, with the expectation that paradoxical surprises await those who will look further and deeper, with the clear plurality of values and concerns, with the failure of simple slogans, theories, and expectations – whatever else we can say about it, morality is neither simple, dogmatic, rosy, nor boring.

Almost by definition a moral paradox requires that we keep trying to make sense of it, to understand what is going on and what it means. The emerging picture, of a moral reality and moral understanding deeply imbued with paradoxes but nevertheless malleable to reason, invites further work on this subject. In this spirit, it seems wrong to conclude our discussion.

Postscript: The Future and Moral Paradox

Books have not so much served me for instruction as exercise.

Michel de Montaigne, *Essays*

There are good reasons to think that we are on the verge of radical changes in human capacities and circumstances, in ways that are bound to affect our morality. New technologies will make obsolete many of our commonsense assumptions about human nature and society. We do not know the full potential for such changes, and understand very little about their nature and implications, yet can be certain that they will be great.

Genetic engineering, nanotechnology, and the integration of the biological and the mechanical will enhance human cognitive, physical, and emotional capacities. If people can be modified (or modify themselves) radically and repeatedly, questions about identity, choice, value, agency, and responsibility will be transformed in extreme ways. Another set of issues concerns membership in the moral community. While our moral world has so far been populated by human beings and, at the margin, other animals, new super (or 'trans')-human, sub-human, and dubiously-human (e.g. robotic) beings will people our future societies, requiring thoroughly new ways of thinking about topics such as respect for persons, the sanctity of the body, violence, gender, and equality. Technologies of surveillance, control, manipulation, communication, and knowledge (e.g. as to when people are lying) should redraw the role of personal conscience and self-control versus social forces, and bring up acute questions about the need to safeguard identity, privacy, and autonomy. The eradication of disease and the availability of technologies for blocking aging processes and for body-replacement, and the great ensuing increase in life span, will transform our notions of career, opportunity, success and failure, and the family. New chemical and virtual-reality capacities for the safe and continuous inducement of pleasure will transform human experience. These are but a few examples of the types of topics and problems that a future ethics will have to deal with.

How do such far-reaching prospects matter to our concern with moral paradoxes? First, we can ask how they will affect the paradoxes uncovered in this book. Some of them may be drastically altered, or even eliminated. If there is much less need for most types of human labor, the paradox of Beneficial Retirement should matter less. The paradoxes dealing with punishment may be thrown out by more efficient ways of preventing crime, either through people's increased ability to manage their own desires, or through enhanced social control. However, even these paradoxes are likely to remain relevant for a long time. Moreover, the deeper perplexities for moral thinking brought out by such paradoxes (e.g. concerning the role of integrity, or of fear and manipulation) should persist. Other paradoxes are likely to remain with us in more familiar ways. Morality and Moral Worth is liable to become only more acute if human life improves in a utopian manner. It is hard to think about a recognizably human world in which the antinomy of the Paradox of Moral Complaint will lose its salience; or one in which misfortune will never prove fortunate. Those paradoxes where a normative component is paramount are also likely to stay relevant: the Paradox of the Baseline will matter to egalitarians, even though (as noted above) the beings who might require equalizing – or not – will be very different from those we deal with today. The moral questions brought about by reflection on the similarity of blackmail to other social practices are also likely to remain pertinent, irrespective of technological change.

Postscript: The Future and Moral Paradox

A more remarkable consequence of the radical and swift changes is likely to be the emergence of entirely new paradoxes. Let us consider one example, the issue I call "*Teflon immorality.*" This concerns the ways in which people can act immorally yet, for various reasons, be beyond the reach of moral (and legal) accountancy. The issue has mattered since the beginning of human society, for wrongdoers have always sought to escape capture. But we can see that if a wrongdoer will indeed become capable of easily transforming him or herself into someone else (through erasing old memories and implanting new ones, for instance), then the issue of accountability will become drastically more severe. After all, according to our current moral standards, after the transformation there will not remain anyone who can be called to account. That would put morality in an absurd predicament. This is not the place to examine such prospects at length, yet we can already see the outline of some of the issues that will keep explorers of future moral paradoxes busy.

Moral philosophy tends to be conservative. Just as it has neglected moral paradoxes, it has hardly begun to confront the prospect for change in the human condition, although we are entering an age of enormous human power over ourselves and of dynamic uncertainty. The emergence of fundamentally new options, the scope and pace of unpredictable and unwieldy change, and the collapse of old certainties, are likely to produce antinomies and absurdities, and to make the future more paradoxical. There is no easier way of making oneself seem a fool in the eyes of posterity than by trying to predict the future. Yet while it is impossible now to predict the details, there will be "future paradoxes," and it seems very likely that in the future we will have to cope with a highly paradoxical environment. This means that getting used to moral paradoxes, and reflecting on how we can cope with them, becomes particularly important.

We may be comforted by the reasonable expectation that in the future people's intelligence will also be much enhanced, so that they will be able both to recognize and to deal better with new moral paradoxes.

The very existence or prevalence of paradoxes will often depend on social choices: we may be able to predict that if we permitted the deployment of technology X, paradoxical consequences of type Y would likely emerge. Even today we have some choice about the incidence of paradoxes, as we saw in the meta-paradox (Chapter 11), when we asked whether it was good or bad that certain paradoxes exist, and whether we should try to limit or enhance them. But although the future will surely close certain possibilities, it will probably also provide much greater power of choice on such matters. In this way as well, the sort of work that we have been doing in this book matters beyond what it teaches us about our current moral world. Just because the future is likely to be so different, and even more paradoxical, we need to practice dealing with paradoxes, and try to prepare for the paradoxicality to come.

References

Arneson, Richard (1989) Equality and equality of opportunity for welfare. *Philosophical Studies* 56, 77–93.

—— (2000) Luck egalitarianism and prioritarianism. *Ethics* 110, 339–49.

Benatar, David (2006) *Better Never to Have Been*. Clarendon Press, Oxford.

Brams, Steven J. (1976) *Paradoxes in Politics*. The Free Press, New York.

Clark, Michael (1994) There is no paradox of blackmail. *Analysis* 54, 54–61.

—— (2002) *Paradoxes from A to Z*. Routledge, London.

Cohen, G. A. (1989) On the currency of egalitarian justice. *Ethics* 99, 906–44.

Cohen, L. Jonathan (1981) Who is starving whom? *Theoria* 47, 65–81.

Feinberg, Joel (1988) The paradox of blackmail. *Ratio Juris* 11, 83–95.

—— (1992) Wrongful life and the counterfactual element in harming. *Freedom and Fulfilment*. Princeton University Press, Princeton.

Fletcher, George P. (1993) Blackmail: the paradigmatic crime. *University of Pennsylvania Law Review* 141, 1617–38.

Gawande, Atul (2004) The bell curve. *New Yorker* <http://www.newyorker.com/printables/fact/041206fa_fact>

Goleman, Daniel (1985) *Vital Lies, Simple Truths*. Simon & Schuster, New York.

Gorr, Michael (1992) Liberalism and the paradox of blackmail. *Philosophy and Public Affairs* 21, 43–66.

Greenspan, Patricia S. (1980) A case of mixed feelings: ambivalence and the logic of emotion. In Amélie Oksenberg Rorty (ed.), *Explaining Emotions*. University of California Press, Berkeley.

Hart, H. L. A. (1970) *Punishment and Responsibility*. Clarendon Press, Oxford.

Heyd, David (1992) *Genethics*. University of California Press, Berkeley.

Hurka, Thomas (1993) *Perfectionism*. Oxford University Press, New York.

James, William (1982) The moral equivalent of war. *Essays in Religion and Morality*. Harvard University Press, Cambridge, Mass.

Kagan, Shelley (1989) *The Limits of Morality*. Clarendon Press, Oxford.

Kamm, F. M. (1993) *Morality, Mortality*, vol. 1. Oxford University Press, New York.

Kant, Immanuel (1986) *Groundwork of the Metaphysics of Morals*, trans. H. J. Paton as *The Moral Law*. Hutchinson, London.

Kavka, Gregory S. (1987) *Moral Paradoxes of Nuclear Deterrence*. Cambridge University Press, Cambridge.

Klein, Martha (1990) *Determinism, Blameworthiness and Deprivation*. Oxford University Press, Oxford.

Lenman, James (2007) Why I have no plans to retire: in defense of moderate professional complacency. *Ratio*, forthcoming.

Levi, Primo (1987) *If This is a Man*. Abacus, London.

Lindgren, James (1984) Unravelling the paradox of blackmail. *Columbia Law Review* 84, 670–717.

Lippert-Rasmussen, Kasper (2004) Smilansky's baseline objection to choice-egalitarianism. *SATS: Nordic Journal of Philosophy* 5, 147–50.

Lukes, Steven (1985) Taking morality seriously. In Ted Honderich (ed.), *Morality and Objectivity*. Routledge & Kegan Paul, London.

Mack, Eric (1982) In defense of blackmail. *Philosophical Studies* 41, 273–84.

McMahan, Jeff (1985) Deterrence and deontology. In Russell Hardin, John J. Mearsheimer, Gerald Dworkin, and Robert E. Goodin (eds.), *Nuclear Deterrence Ethics and Strategy*. University of Chicago Press, Chicago.

Manor, Tal (2005) Inequality: mind the gap! A reply to Smilansky's paradox of the baseline. *Analysis* 65, 265–8.

Murphy, Jeffrie G. (1980) Blackmail: a preliminary inquiry. *Monist* 63, 156–71.

Nagel, Thomas (1998) Concealment and exposure. *Philosophy and Public Affairs* 27, 3–30.

New, Christopher (1992) Time and punishment. *Analysis* 52, 35–40.

—— (1995) Punishing times: reply to Smilansky. *Analysis* 55, 60–2.

Olin, Doris (2003) *Paradox*. Acumen, Chesham.

Parfit, Derek (1984) *Reasons and Persons*. Clarendon Press, Oxford.

—— (1986) Overpopulation and the quality of life. In Peter Singer (ed.), *Applied Ethics*. Oxford University Press, Oxford.

Poundstone, William (1990) *Labyrinths of Reason*. Anchor Books, New York.

Priest, Graham (2006) *In Contradiction*. 2nd edn. Clarendon Press, Oxford.

Quine, W. V. (1976) *The Ways of Paradox and Other Essays*. Harvard University Press, Cambridge, Mass.

Rakowski, Eric (1991) *Equal Justice*. Clarendon Press, Oxford.

Rawls, John (2000) *A Theory of Justice*. Rev. edn. Harvard University Press, Cambridge, Mass.

Rescher, Nicholas (2001) *Paradoxes: Their Roots, Range, and Resolution*. Open Court, Chicago.

Sainsbury, R. M. (1996) *Paradoxes*. 2nd edn. Cambridge University Press, Cambridge.

Singer, Peter (1972) Famine, affluence, and morality. *Philosophy and Public Affairs* 1, 229–43.

Smilansky, Saul (1990) Utilitarianism and the "punishment" of the innocent: the general problem. *Analysis* 50, 29–33.

—— (1992) Two apparent paradoxes about justice and the severity of punishment. *Southern Journal of Philosophy* 30, 123–8.

—— (1994a) The ethical advantages of hard determinism. *Philosophy and Phenomenological Research* 54, 355–63.

—— (1994b) Fortunate misfortune. *Ratio* 7, 153–63.

—— (1994c) On practicing what we preach. *American Philosophical Quarterly* 31, 73–9.

—— (1994d) The time to punish. *Analysis* 54, 50–3.

—— (1995a) May we stop worrying about blackmail? *Analysis* 55, 116–20.

—— (1995b) Nagel on the grounds for compensation. *Public Affairs Quarterly* 9, 63–73.

—— (1996a) Responsibility and desert: defending the connection. *Mind* 105, 157–63.

—— (1996b) The connection between responsibility and desert: the crucial distinction. *Mind* 105, 385–6.

References

—— (1997a) Egalitarian justice and the importance of the free will problem. *Philosophia* 25, 153–61.

—— (1997b) Preferring not to have been born. *Australasian Journal of Philosophy* 75, 241–7.

—— (2000) *Free Will and Illusion*. Oxford University Press, Oxford.

—— (2001) Blackmail. *Encyclopaedia of Ethics*. 2nd edn. Routledge, London.

—— (2003) Choice-egalitarianism and the paradox of the baseline. *Analysis* 63, 146–51.

—— (2004) Reply to Kasper Lippert-Rasmussen on the paradox of the baseline. *SATS: Nordic Journal of Philosophy* 5, 151–3.

—— (2005a) On not being sorry about the morally bad. *Philosophy* 80, 261–5.

—— (2005b) The paradoxical relationship between morality and moral worth. *Metaphilosophy* 36, 490–500.

—— (2005c) The paradox of beneficial retirement. *Ratio* 18, 332–7.

—— (2005d) Choice-egalitarianism and the paradox of the baseline: a reply to Manor. *Analysis* 265, 333–7.

—— (2006a) The paradox of moral complaint. *Utilitas*, 18, 284–90.

—— (2006b) Some thoughts on terrorism, complaint, and the self-reflexive and relational nature of morality. *Philosophia*, 34, 65–74.

—— (2007) The paradox of beneficial retirement: a reply to Lenman. *Ratio*, forthcoming.

Sorensen, Roy (2003) *A Brief History of the Paradox*. Oxford University Press, New York.

Statman, Daniel, ed. (1993) *Moral Luck*. SUNY Press, Albany, NY.

Taylor, Shelley E. (1989) *Positive Illusions*. Basic Books, New York.

Temkin, Larry S. (2003) Egalitarianism defended. *Ethics* 113, 764–82.

Velleman, J. David (2000) Well-being and time. *The Possibility of Practical Reason*. Oxford University Press, Oxford.

Williams, Bernard (1973a) Ethical consistency. *Problems of the Self*. Cambridge University Press, Cambridge.

—— (1973b) A critique of utilitarianism. In J. J. C. Smart and Bernard Williams, *Utilitarianism: For and Against*. Cambridge University Press, Cambridge.

—— (1985) *Ethics and the Limits of Philosophy*. Fontana, London.

—— (1995) Resenting one's own existence. *Making Sense of Humanity*. Cambridge University Press, Cambridge.

Index

absurd(ity) 22, 115–19, 128,
132–3
and choice-egalitarianism 71–2,
74, 76
and moral worth 82, 88–9
and paradox 3–5
and punishment 38, 40–1
Aristotle 69
Arneson, Richard 68

Benatar, David 109
blackmail
conceptual paradox of 44–5
definition of 42–3
substantive paradox of 45–9
Brams, Steven J. 10

choice 19, 41, 84–5, 124, 130,
132
and blackmail 45, 48
and egalitarianism 67–76
and non-punishment 51–2,
55–8
Cicero 53
Clark, Michael 1, 44
Cohen, G. A. 68
Cohen, L. Jonathan 84
consequentialism see utilitarianism
contractual ethics 30, 48, 131

crime and criminals see punishment
cynicism 46, 79, 97

deontology 30, 34, 46, 48, 53,
69, 78, 90, 95, 131
desert 27, 63, 65, 93–4, 124
and choice-egalitarianism 67–8,
71–6
and Fortunate Misfortune
16–17, 19–20
and punishment 33–41, 52–3
Dostoevsky, Fyodor 18

effort 8–9, 27, 29, 129–30
and choice-egalitarianism 70–2,
74
and Fortunate Misfortune 12,
15–16, 19, 21
and moral worth 77–89
Einstein, Albert 131
equality and egalitarianism 21,
36–7, 62, 67–76, 116–18,
124–5
existential paradox 4–5, 41, 116,
121, 123–4, 132
Existential Test 26

Feinberg, Joel 47, 102
Fletcher, George P. 47

Fortunate Misfortune 11–22, 60, 77, 105, 114, 123, 125–6, 129–32
free will 1, 9n, 16, 55–6, 60, 68–9, 86

Goleman, Daniel 29
Gorr, Michael 47
Greenspan, Patricia S. 62

Hart, H. L. A. 52, 56
Heyd, David 101–2
Hobbes, Thomas 49
Holocaust, the 20, 61, 79, 103–5
Hurka, Thomas 110
hypocrisy 46, 62, 66, 97

integrity 6, 30, 39–41, 93, 119, 129–30, 132

James, William 87

Kagan, Shelley 78
Kamm, F. M. 111
Kant, Immanuel 53, 78
Kavka, Gregory 10n, 56–7
Klein, Martha 37
knowledge 5, 15, 48, 110, 116, 120, 125–8, 130
    and obligation to retire 26–8
    as potentially harmful or dangerous 28–9, 61, 115, 126

law, the 42–9, 52–3, 80, 83, 92, 96, 117
Lenman, James 32n
Levi, Primo 20
Lindgren, James 47
Lippert-Rasmussen, Kasper 74

luck 29, 31, 61, 85, 103
    and egalitarianism 67–76
    and Fortunate Misfortune 13–16, 18, 21
Lukes, Steven 80

Mack, Eric 46
McMahan, Jeff 56–7
Manor, Tal 75–6n
Mill, John Stuart 79
moral paradox(es)
    like black holes in moral universe 132
    concern with not common 2
    how discovered 51, 59–60, 100
    and life 9, 114–15, 120–1, 129, 133–7
    and meta-ethics 8, 127–8
    and nonmoral paradoxes 125
    and "over-commitment" 115–16
    reasons for neglect of 2–3
    where come from 119–20
Murphy, Jeffrie G. 47

Nagel, Thomas 29
New, Christopher 55
Nietzsche, Friedrich 18, 80
9/11 63

Olin, Doris 1, 10n

paradox(es)
    definition of 3–4
    as haikus of philosophy 3
    solutions do not dispel 19, 128–9
    types of 4–5
    see also moral paradox(es)
Parfit, Derek 10n, 22n, 61, 102
philosophy 2, 8, 125, 132
    and moral paradoxes 3, 113–14, 129, 134–7

143

Plato 10n
Poundstone, William 1, 5
pragmatic considerations 25, 83,
    87, 114–15, 118
  and blackmail 46–9
  and choice-egalitarianism 71,
    74–5
  and not being sorry 61, 64
  and punishment 38–9, 41,
    54–5
Priest, Graham 127
punishment 24, 33–41, 50–8,
    62–3, 115–20, 124
  compared to love 38
  and moral complaint 91–9
  over-punishment compared with
    pre-punishment 55–6

Quine, W. V. 3, 4, 10n

racism 20–1, 62–3
Rakowski, Eric 68
Rawls, John 95
reason and rationality 5, 8–9, 81,
    126, 132–3
  and Fortunate Misfortune
    14–15, 20–2
  and non-punishment 52, 54
  and preferring not to have been
    born 100–12
Rescher, Nicholas 1, 116
risk 31, 51–2, 54–5, 67–8, 80,
    83–5, 114–15

Sainsbury, R. M. 1, 4, 10n
Singer, Peter 84
Sorensen, Roy 1, 10n
sorry *for* and sorry *that*, distinction
    between 60–6
Statman, Daniel 21

Taylor, Shelley E. 29
Teflon immorality 136
Temkin, Larry 68
terrorism 63, 83, 91–9
tragedy 20, 31, 38, 116, 132

utilitarianism and consequentialism
    8–9, 18, 30, 62, 78, 84, 102,
    111
  and blackmail 42, 48–9
  and punishment 33–8, 50–4
  see also pragmatic considerations

vegetarianism 87
Velleman, David J. 22n
victim, being a 30, 36–7, 43–5,
    104–5, 114
  and Fortunate Misfortune 16, 21
  and moral complaint 91–4, 96
  and non-punishment 50, 53–6
  and not being sorry 63–4
virtue ethics 30, 48, 61, 63–6,
    78–81, 131

Williams, Bernard 30, 80–1,
    100–2, 105, 107–9